…RNELSEN
…IOR
…LISH
…RARY

Envisioning Other Worlds: Science Fiction and Dystopia

Cornelsen

Envisioning Other worlds: Science Fiction and Dystopia

Textwahl und Annotationen: Christian Ludwig
Verlagsredaktion: Neil Porter
Umschlaggestaltung: Cornelsen Design
Umschlagfoto: Fotolia/grandfailure
Layout und technische Umsetzung: Annika Preyhs für Buchgestaltung +, Berlin

www.cornelsen.de

1. Auflage, 1. Druck 2018

Alle Drucke dieser Auflage sind inhaltlich unverändert und können im Unterricht nebeneinander verwendet werden.

Druck: H. Heenemann, Berlin

ISBN 978-3-06-036163-2

PEFC
PEFC/04-31-1156

PEFC zertifiziert
Dieses Produkt stammt aus nachhaltig bewirtschafteten Wäldern und kontrollierten Quellen.

www.pefc.de

CONTENTS

Abbreviations and Annotations

adj	adjective	infml	informal
adv	adverb	n	noun
AE	American English	pl	plural
derog	derogatory	sb.	somebody
e.g.	exempli gratia; for example	sl	slang
esp.	especially	sth.	something
etc.	et cetera; and so on	usu.	usually
fml	formal	v	verb

The annotations are arranged chronologically; the first time a word is used is where you will find it explained.

TO THE STUDENT

The idea of a utopia – a perfect place where people can live in peace and happiness – has fascinated humanity for centuries. The term 'utopia' was coined from the Greek by Sir Thomas More for his 1516 book *Utopia*, in which he described a fictional island society in the south Atlantic Ocean. The word comes from Greek σu ('not') and τόπος ('place'), and means 'no-place'. However, due to the similarity in sound between σu and the Greek εu ('good'), the term utopia came to be used to describe a fictional society that is intended to be viewed as better than contemporary society.

From the 19th century onwards, more and more dystopias, strongly rooted in utopian fiction, were published. In contrast to utopian literature, dystopias almost always draw on current developments for their social models. The writer criticizes his or her own society by demonstrating how certain trends may develop. This term is referred to as 'extrapolation', in that the writer extrapolates elements of contemporary society in order to serve as a warning of future developments.

Some of the most famous examples of dystopian fiction are Aldous Huxley's *Brave New World* (1932), George Orwell's *1984* (1949), Ray Bradbury's *Fahrenheit 451* (1953) and Margret Atwood's *The Handmaid's Tale* (1985), which have all been adapted into films. More recently, there has been an increase in dystopian literature for young adults. Like other dystopian novels, they too are often set in future societies, characterized by totalitarian and oppressive governments, economic ruthlessness, environmental disasters and technological developments which have led to dehumanization and deindividualization. Young adult dystopias often feature female teenage protagonists who, as they become adults, find themselves at odds with elements of their society and, despite their age and gender, gradually develop into symbols of resistance, thereby threatening the continued existence of the society in its current form. Julie Bertagna's *Exodus* (2002) and Saci Lloyd's *The Carbon Diaries 2015* (2009) are good examples of how female protagonists have to come to terms with the changes in their lives when the societies around them change radically. As young women, they are forced to take on more active roles to save themselves and the people around them.

However, this collection of fiction is not only about young adult dystopian fiction but also about science fiction, a genre popular in computer games, films and TV series. While science often only plays a marginal role in young adult dystopian fiction, many works of science fiction explore the potential consequences of innovations in science, often also paying attention to how science can influence the development of both society and the individual. Many of the stories collected here are examples of this. Ray Bradbury's 1952 short story 'A Sound of Thunder' takes the reader to the year 2055, when commercial time travel has become a practical reality. The protagonist books a hunting safari 65 million years in the past to kill a Tyrannosaurus Rex. By stepping off the tourist anti-gravity metal path, he accidentally causes changes to the future.

James Tiptree, Jr's (the pen name of American writer Alice Sheldon) science-fiction novella *The Girl Who Was Plugged in* (1973) is set in a dystopian future and tells the story of 17-year-old Philadelphia who is turned into a cyborg and controls a perfect female body via remote control in a world ruled by corporations. Ursula Le Guin's short story 'Solitude' (1994) deals with a protagonist who remembers her childhood on the planet Eleven-Soro, whose population, once technologically advanced, has reverted to a simpler lifestyle. Together with her mother, an ethnologist, and brother, she experiences growing up in a world that is characterized by strict gender separation and an extreme sense of individuality, allowing the reader to examine the nature of family relationships and bonding through the eyes of a young teenage girl. The short story 'Lost Memory' (1952) by Peter Phillips is also concerned with the nature of human relations and cultural differences. While most science-fiction stories are told from a human perspective, 'Lost Memory' shows how our actions are defined by our viewpoint by taking the perspective of post-human beings when an injured human astronaut wakes up in a world of robots. Initially created by the computer of an automated spaceship, the robots have no concept of human existence.

Isaac Asimov's story 'The Bicentennial Man' (1976) questions the boundaries between humans and machines. It follows the story of the robot butler Andrew who works not only to become an anatomically fully functional android but to be accepted as a human being against all prevailing human prejudices. In the end, he even decides to give up his immortality to achieve his desire to be legally recognized as a human. In the second poem in this volume, 'The Migration of Darkness' (1979), Peter Payack contemplates what would happen if darkness were not simply the absence of light but an entity that possessed physical substance.

Apart from learning more about how writers envision the future, you will also learn more about the importance and role of language in society. We need language not only to express our feelings but also our individuality. Therefore, language plays an important role in many works of science fiction and dystopian fiction. Some authors create their own languages or words, often to describe objects or concepts which do not (yet) exist. Moreover, unknown words make our reading experience more alien and show us how difficult it can be to understand people from foreign cultures if we do not have the necessary empathy. One example of how the restriction of language is used by governments to humiliate individuals and subdue them to totalitarian rule can be seen in Jeffrey McDaniel's poem 'The Quiet World' (1998). It takes the reader to an undefined future in which the use of language itself, often considered the main sign of human exceptionalism, has been limited to a certain number of words. Although the characters in the poem know that their situation is inescapable, they are not willing to give up expressing their love for each other, despite the repression of the government.

In the present collection you will find some of the most powerful pieces of science fiction and young adult dystopian writing. All of the stories will give you the opportunity to explore the two genres in poetry and prose and also to learn more about a quite recent but nevertheless very popular visual medium – the graphic novel. Although all the stories are about the future, they will also help you identify present issues and problems. When reading one or all of the texts, the following questions will support you in identifying some of their central themes as well as reflecting on how the future as depicted can help you to understand the present:

- What are the central issues of the story?
- What does the future tell you about the present?
- To what extent can you already identify developments in our contemporary society that may lead to the future depicted in the story?

We wish you enjoyment in getting to know this collection of writings and authors.

Peter Payack

The Migration of Darkness

Peter Payack is an acclaimed American poet and has published over 1,500 poems. "The Migration of Darkness" received the Rhysling Award for the best science-fiction poem in 1980. Payack lives and teaches in Cambridge, Massachusetts, and was elected the city's first Poet Populist, a reflection of his unconventional approach to poetry. He has done various things to gain public attention for poetry, from sandblasting poems into walls to creating Phone-a-Poem.

Before you read the poem, imagine darkness was a living being. How would you describe it? What would be its relationship with daylight?

Each evening, shortly after sunset,
darkness covers the land.
    Having mystified thinkers for millennia,
    the mechanism for this occurrence
    has now been identified: migration.
Darkness, it has been found, is composed
of an almost infinite number of particles,
which roost[1] and reproduce up north
where they have fewer natural enemies:
    Forest fires, lampposts[2], lasers, blazing[3] sunlight,
    torches, candles, lighthouses, limelight[4], and electricity
    are relatively rare in the polar regions.
These lightweight bits of darkness
flock together and fly south each evening
to more fertile land in a never-ending search
for an abundant[5] food supply.

1 roost: rest, sleep **2** lamppost: *Laternenpfahl* **3** blazing: *prall, gleißend*
4 limelight: *Rampenlicht* **5** abundant: more than enough

With the coming of the rising sun,
they return to their northern nesting grounds.
However, not all specks[1] of darkness migrate.
Some that are less adventurous
    or downright lazy
choose to stay behind.
These covey[2] together, in varying numbers,
seeking shelter from the strong sunlight
    by gathering under leafy trees, behind
    large rocks, and underneath umbrellas;
    hiding in alleys, between parked cars,
    in caves, and inside empty pockets.
These clusters are perceived by us as shadows.
They have a somewhat shorter life span
than those which migrate.

1 speck: spot **2** covey: flock

Julie Bertagna

The Rising Waves

Julia Bertagna was born in 1962 in Kilmarnock, Scotland, and grew up in Glasgow. Bertagna holds a degree in literature and has worked as an editor, teacher and journalist. She published her first novel, *The Spark Gap,* in 1996. Her highly acclaimed science-fiction novel *Exodus* (2002), from which the following extract is taken, took her almost ten years to write. It won several awards and was followed by two sequels, *Zenith* (2007) and *Aurora* (2011). Bertagna works as a full-time writer in Glasgow.

What does the word 'exodus' mean? Which other book has the word 'exodus' in it? Explain what the book is about. Now write down your own definition of the word.

Research which countries are most at risk from climate change. What might happen to the inhabitants of these countries?

WING

Midwinter 2099

Earth spins. And Wing, the high island, is hurled into the sunless shadow of night.

It's just a minute past three.

The people of Wing are gathering in what's left of their village. Downhill, the salty, sea-lashed[1] streets run straight into churning[2], cold-boiled ocean. The oldest islanders can remember a time when Wing's folding hills sheered away to sandstone cliffs that plunged on to a wide and rocky shore. The clifftops were still visible at ebb tide last summer, haunting the waves with their dark shadows.

1 sea-lashed: hit by the sea with violent force **2** churn: *sich heftig bewegen*

Now it's all ocean.

The people turn their backs to the waves and head uphill through the field of windmills. The slow grind of the wind blades is only a hoarse[1] whisper in this evening of rare midwinter calm. The Pole Star glitters overhead, a tiny torch that guides the islanders to a plateau high in the hills where eleven tall slabs[2] of stone stand in an ancient circle. As the last of the sun's rays fade upon the ocean and night cloaks the island, the people banish all thought of the rising waves that surround them.

Just as their ancestors did, for time out of my mind, they stand in the middle of the standing stones to celebrate the midwinter solstice[3]. Excitement fills the air as fireballs on ropes are set alight. Throwers grasp the long ropes and spin the flaming balls of straw round and round, then send each one hurtling high into the sky. Whoops and cheers echo all across Wing as the darkness is shredded with a cascade of falling stars to mark the death of the old year's sun.

Now a huge wheel, an ancient symbol of the fiery revolution of the stars, is set ablaze and sent whirling downhill. The islanders roar with delight as the fire-wheel flames a great track through the dark, all down the hillside and across the waves, burning itself out like a fading supernova upon the black ocean.

The darkness is absolute. People huddle closer together as it engulfs[4] them, glancing up at the flickering stars for reassurance.

Old Tain feels his way to the centre of the standing stones. He has seen nearly eighty midwinter fires, more than anyone else on the island. He lifts out the ember[5] that he has brought from his own fireside in a clay pot and light the stack of dried peat[6] and tindery[7] driftwood[8] at the centre of the standing stones. After a while the fire begins to spark and to crackle. The people of Wing cheer as light breaks the dark, heralding the new sun that is about to be born.

1 hoarse: *heiser* **2** slab: a thick flat piece of hard material **3** midwinter solstice: *Wintersonnenwende* **4** engulf sb./sth.: swallow sb./sth. up **5** ember: *Glut* **6** peat: *Torf* **7** tindery: highly inflammable **8** driftwood: *Treibholz*

Tain climbs upon the twelfth stone that lies fallen inside the circle. When he raises a hand the others fall quiet.

'Happy New Year!' he cries. 'Tomorrow we'll see the first sun of a whole new century!'

Tain eyes the happy crowd, knowing they are all anxious to eat and drink and party. He hesitates and the lines that plough[1] his face deepen.

'Maybe the new century will bring us a miracle,' he declares. 'We'll need one to save us from that rising sea ... But what if the miracle we all hope for doesn't happen? Listen to me. We must begin to plan for the future. We must look out to the world beyond these islands –'

'Oh, Tain, no!' cries Brenna, a small, apple-cheeked woman with a noisy brood of young children. She smiles at him to soften her rebuke. 'We don't want to think of such things on a night like this!'

'This is the very night we should think of the future,' Tain responds.

'The children are all here. I don't want them frightened,' argues Brenna, her smile fading.

'The children I'm thinking of. It's their future that's at stake if the sea keeps rising and we do nothing,' growls Tain.

An angry muttering starts in the crowd. Brenna's right, people agree, no one wants to think about the sea tonight. The anger swells and voices rise. A few islanders try to defend Tain but they are drowned out by the many who, like Brenna, just want to celebrate and forget. People begin to turn away for home. But a girl, cheeks blazing[2], dark eyes flashing, her long hair glistening[3] like a midnight ocean, jumps up on to the toppled stone to stand beside the old man and pleads with the crowd to stay and listen to him.

There's a lull[4] as the islanders halt for a moment, their attention caught by the fiery spirit of the girl, by her sheer energy as she

1 plough sth. [plaʊ]: *etwas durchziehen* **2** blazing: red due to heat **3** glistening: *glitzernd* **4** lull: *Gesprächspause*

stands upon her stone platform like an avenging angel[1], haloed[2] by the flames of the sunfire behind her.

Tain takes advantage of the lull to try and calm everyone.

'Peace now!' he urges, in pacifying but resigned tones. He puts a steadying hand on the girl's shoulder. 'All right, Mara. Let's all calm down and be happy tonight. But before the celebrations begin, we'll join hands around the sunfire and ready ourselves for the future.'

The people regather[3] and a moment of silence falls as they stand cocooned in the light and heat of their sunfire, snug together within a dark, cold world. A hundred hopes and wishes zip skywards with the sparks and smoke.

Now everyone warms up with steaming mugs of mulled beet-wine and fire-baked potatoes before the trek back down the hillside. The midwinter fires of the other islands scatter the ocean with a constellation of tiny lights that mirrors the fiery network of the skies. The procession ends back in the village as the island's church bell peals[4], finding its echo in others across the waves. Wing's narrow, huddled streets are soon full of firelight and feasting and rousing songs that drown out the noise of the ocean, long into the night, as the islanders celebrate the living power of the universe.

But Tain's words linger in the air. The new century will surely bring the miracle we need, the islanders tell each other. Earth may have abandoned others to its swallowing seas – people in far distant lands – but, they claim, that could never happen to us.

Yet, tonight the ocean takes another hungry gulp, reaching further up the hillsides of Wing, ever closer to the village and the farms, towards the very doorsteps of the islanders' homes.

1 avenging angel: *Racheengel* **2** halo sb.: *jdn. mit einem Heiligenschein versehen*
3 regather: *sich neu versammeln* **4** peal: *läuten*

THE SWALLOWING SEA

April 2100

Mara Bell wakens full of restless flutterings[1], as if there's a tiny bird trapped in her heart.

The air is full of the noise of hammers and saws. Quickly, Mara unbolts her window and unlatches the storm shutters[2]. Sunshine explodes into the room. She blinks, stunned and delighted, then leans out of the window and revels[3] in the sensation of fresh air, in the panorama of sea and sky; an endless, electric blue.

Frantic activity fills the island as the people of Wing take their chance, during this rare lull in the weather, to repair the storm-battered barricades.

'Breakfast, Marabell!' her mother's clear, quick voice calls up, merging her two plain names into one beautiful sound like water running stones.

But first, before she does anything else, Mara reaches under her bed for her cyberwizz. The islanders have long abandoned such relics. No one has any use of the old technology now. No one except Mara.

She clicks open the small, solid glove of the cyberwizz, takes out two tiny solar rods that are almost out of power, and lays them on her windowsill to recharge in the sun.

Then Mara flings on her clothes and races downstairs to escape the house she has been trapped in for three interminably long months of storm.

'Hold on, hold on!' Rosemary, her mother, points to the kitchen table with one hand and holds up a hammer in the other. 'I said breakfast, Marabell. Then hammering. Lots of it.'

1 fluttering: *Flattern* **2** shutter: *Fensterladen* **3** revel in sth.: enjoy sth. in an enthusiastic way

Mara ruffles[1] her little brother's blond curls, steals a bit of his toast, then zips out of the door before anyone can stop her. At a safe distance down the hillside she turns to wave at her mother who stands at the door, hands on her slim hips, her short, dark hair ruffled by the wind as she shakes her head and brandishes[2] the hammer. But the grin on her face matches her daughter's. Rosemary knows nothing will keep Mara indoors on such a morning. They also both know the storm clouds could easily be back before the sun sets, so every second outside is a gift.

Mara races down through the sloping field of windmills and solar panes. Free at last! It feels glorious. The world's wind sweeps across the ocean and wraps her in billows[3] that swirl up her dark fall of hair. The morning sun on her skin is bliss. The never-ending blue of sky and ocean is heaven to her eyes after months of dim lantern-light and staring at walls.

When she reaches the hump-backed road bridge where the old red telephone box sits alongside a storm-bent bus stop sign, she pauses. Once upon a time Wing had all sorts of vehicles – buses, cars, motorbikes, lorries and tractors. Mara has seen old photographs of them. But when the fuel ran out, over half a century ago, they were all recycled for other uses. Nowadays, the only vehicle Wing ever sees is the rusted shell of a car that's sometimes swept ashore and eagerly melted down[4] for its metal. But the islanders could not bear to recycle the metal telephone box or the bus stop sign. They were part of the island's landscape, every bit as much as the church or the standing stones.

Mara feels a tremor of fear as she sees how much the ocean has risen over the winter. The hump-backed bridge runs straight into the waves. The sea can't come any closer, surely. The thought is too awful, so to put it out of her mind she runs to the edge of the waves to see what the storm has cast up.

1 ruffle sth.: *etwas zerzausen* **2** brandish sth.: *etwas schwingen* **3** billow: *Woge*
4 melt sth. down: *etwas einschmelzen*

A shoe! Mara rushes over to grab this precious bit of flotsam[1] that the ocean has flung upon the grass. If she could just find one more. She looks down at her burst, heavily-patched trainers, hand-me-downs from her mother and grandmother. She desperately needs new shoes and doesn't care how mismatched they are. She plans to rip each shoe apart and make herself a brand new pair. Meticulously, Mara searches until she finds a real bounty[2] – a leather bag caught in a large branch at the sea's edge.

Leather and driftwood – a real find! She'll give the driftwood to old Tain; he'll understand that she and her family need the leather so badly. But Tain will be able to do plenty with a good lump of wood like this. Mara drags the hefty branch up the hillside to the old man's cottage, where the sound of hammering echoes, as it does from every other house on the island.

'Well!' he grins down from the ladder where he is securing a ripped storm shutter to an upstairs window. 'So you've found a treasure!'

Tain descends the ladder, slowly but with more agility, Mara judges, than you'd ever expect from a man of almost eighty. He hugs Mara and holds her by the shoulders to look at her.

'You've managed to bloom without sunlight,' he tells her. 'You've grown into a young woman over the winter.'

'Well, I've just turned fifteen.'

Tain nods, smiling. 'I didn't forget. Your present's inside.'

'That wasn't a hint,' laughs Mara.

Tain examines her finds with interest.

'The leather –' Mara begins, apologetically, but Tain cuts in.

'That young brother of yours will be bursting out of his shoes like nobody's business and yours look like they could do with a good bit of mending too. No, Mara, keep your treasure. I'm just fine.'

He stamps his extremely tatty[3] but sturdy[4] boots on the ground.

'I brought the wood for you though,' Mara insists. 'I dragged it all the way up here so don't tell me you won't take it. Look at my hands!'

1 flotsam: *Treibgut* **2** bounty: treasure **3** tatty: *schäbig* **4** sturdy: *robust*

She holds up her palms, raw from hauling the great branch.

'I'll finish off that shutter for you.' Mara picks the hammer from the grass and climbs the ladder.

'I'll boil us up some tea then,' says Tain and he looks suddenly weary. Fit or not, thinks Mara, he really is too old to be doing these repairs himself. But he won't let any of the other islanders help him – a mixture of pride and a selfless awareness of the struggle each household has to maintain a roof over its own head when the storm season hits.

Tain's stone cottage was built over two centuries ago. The old man was born in it, as was his mother, and her mother before her. The rest of its long history is lost in time. Tain likes to slam a hand upon his home and declare that its rock-solid walls will last till the end of the Earth. Now he stares out at the enclosing sea with eyes that have watched the horizon for the best part of a century, as if he is no longer sure.

Mara loves this cottage as much as Tain does. It's her second home. When she was little, Tain took her under his wing and let her tag along with him as he stacked the peat and fed the goats and turned the cheeses, calling her his little helper, though really it was Tain who was helping Mara, making her glow inside, making her feel important and special when her father was so busy with the farm and her mother all tied up with baby Corey.

'People say it won't happen,' Mara bursts out. 'They say the ocean will settle again in the summer and we'll be safe.'

Now Tain's eyes brew up[1] a look that's as wild as a turbulent sea. He juts out[2] his great crappy chin and puts out a hand to touch the stone wall of his cottage. Silently, he seems to challenge the mighty ocean before he turns on Mara.

'But you can use your eyes, Mara, even if they can't!' he cries. 'You're not a child any more and I won't lie to you. We all have to open our eyes now and look beyond this godforsaken place at the edge of the Earth.'

1 brew sth.: *(hier) etwas annehmen* **2** jut sth. out: stick sth. out

Mara's heart sinks as she nails the shutter back in place. She has never heard Tain talk in such a way. His family, like hers, has lived on Wing for generations, longer than anyone can remember. Tain has never left the island; he only ever speaks of his heritage with pride. Until now.

A fat house spider scuttles on to the storm shutter. Mara halts in mid-swing and lets the spider escape on to the window ledge before she smashes the hammer down. She has never left the island, either – at least, not in reality. Mara travels far in her own, secret way but she never tells anyone about these adventures. They belong to her.

Tain beckons Mara to come down off the ladder. When her feet touch the ground, he takes her by the shoulders and gently but firmly pulls her round to confront the sea.

'Don't you do the same as the others. Don't look away and fool yourself. They're wrong. There's no great miracle going to save us. The only way we'll be saved is to face up to the truth.

Mara's heart sinks even more as she looks across the field of whirling windmills and glinting solar panes to where there was once a long shoreline and road, a harbour and the island's school. Just a few years ago, Mara and her friends went to the school. Then the sea claimed it. Even at midwinter you could still see its flat roof. Now it is completely lost.

To the north is a network of small, craggy islands. Once, they were all joined as a single landmass but over the last century the plains and much of the hills have been swallowed by the sea and now only the peaks remain. Scattered across the slow-churning ocean, they look like bits of storm-tossed litter. Over the last century many islanders have had to shift homes and farms and entire villages up out of reach of the rising ocean – some more than once. Wing, the largest and highest island, is now overcrowded with refugees from its northern neighbours, who have made makeshift homes in the ruins of its ancient stone cottages and farmyard outhouses.

'Oh, Tain!' wails Mara. 'What can we do?'

Mara feels the bird-like fluttering in her heart once again. This time it's not restlessness, but fear.

Tain sighs and juts out his chin. 'We should have done something long before now. It took me long enough to face the truth. But maybe there's still time, if we act now.'

Mara stares out at the ocean, lost in thought. When she turns back to Tain she catches the strange, wistful look he sometimes fixes upon her. Mara knows it's not really to do with her. It's because she looks so like her grandmother did, the girl he grew up with long ago.

'Tea?' she prompts, to bring him back to the present.

'Tea,' he nods, with a shy smile, and they go inside.

Mara munches gratefully on the large, warm, buttery oatcake that Tain hands her. The fresh air and a missed breakfast have made her ravenous[1]. She eats it standing in a pool of sunlight by the open door, reluctant to miss a second of this glorious weather, while Tain stokes the stove and boils up the kettle. Mara finds his peaty brew too strong and bitter so he always makes her mint leaf tea with a spoonful of heather honey[2], which she loves.

'Tell me about you and Granny Mary,' she says, closing her eyes and lifting her face to the sun like a flower, preferring to fill her thoughts with stories of the old days rather than the threat of the future.

'I've told you all the stories,' he says briskly.

Mara debates whether she dare ask the next question – one that she has had plenty of time to wonder about through the long storm months. That wistful[3] look of Tain's when he remembers Granny Mary has made her wonder.

'Did you love her?' she bursts out at last. 'You did, didn't you?'

Tain doesn't answer, just pours out the tea. They sit at the table in silence, amid the bright sunbeams that spill through the open window.

'Ah, it's all far away in the past now, Maram' he says at last.

1 ravenous: very hungry **2** heather honey: *Heidehonig* **3** wistful: *sehnsüchtig*

'But –'

'All over and done with. What we need to think of now is the future.'

Mara's mind is spinning. It's just as she suspected. There was something between Tain and Granny Mary. That must be why he has always taken such a deep, fond interest in her, She knows she is her grandmother's image; all the old people tell her so and she has seen the striking resemblance in photographs of Granny Mary in her youth – the same intense expression and thick, dark sweep of hair; the same long, lean limbs; and even, says her mother, the same restless way of moving.

But no one has ever suggested that Granny Mary was anything other than happily married to Grandpa and they both died when they were old, so how is it possible that Tain –

'Listen to me, Mara.' Tain's voice breaks into her thoughts. 'Your future is not here on Wing. There might be no Wing left soon – or not enough for us all to live on. Your future lies somewhere else in the world.'

The puzzle of her grandmother's past is abandoned for the moment as Mara's mind fills with more urgent questions.

'What's the world beyond here like, Tain? No one ever talks about it.'

Mara thinks of the places she has seen on her secret travels. Amazing places, so strange and different to the familiar land and seascape that surround her. But her travels are not real, they're only electric visions.

'The outside world is a great mystery now,' says Tain. 'That's why we never talk about it.'

'But what do you think?' Mara persists.

Tain sighs heavily. 'I don't know. When the oceans first rose and swallowed the lands, we were all in shock. The supply ships from the mainland suddenly stopped and all our communications systems went down. We were petrified.' He leans forward and Mara sees a tremor of emotion, the reflection of that long ago terror, on his mouth. 'We had no way of knowing what was happening to the rest of the world. And there was so much to do. We had to change our whole way of life, move all our homes and farms far uphill, out of reach of the sea. We had to make ourselves completely self-sufficient in just a few years. All this in the midst of storms like you've never seen. We had barely any time to think of anything beyond ourselves and our own little patch of the world. It was a huge struggle just to survive. But at last, when the seas calmed enough, some of our fishermen set out to see what had happened on the mainland.' Tain pauses again, and the look in his eyes tells Mara he still finds it hard to believe. 'They found nothing but ocean. There were the rocky peaks of what had once been the highlands – solid rock that no one could live on – but no sign of any land. Once we heard that, we turned our thoughts away from the outside world. And that's how we stayed, never looking beyond these islands. Till now.'

Tain grasps Mara's hand in his.

'Mara, the seas are rising again. It happens in surges[1]. Every few decades there's another great meltdown of the ice at the poles and then you get sea surge. I know the pattern – I've seen it before. We've had long, scorching summers these last years and now we're getting the sea surge from the meltdown that the weather has caused. I think the last of the polar icecaps must be melting.'

Last summer the heat had burned the island almost barren[2]. Mara remembers air so hot it shimmered like glass. Days so long and bright the relentless sun hardly slipped from the sky. The sea was a haven[3] then – she lived on the rocks like a mermaid, her wet long hair a long, cool cloak against the sun, endlessly plunging her burning skin into the soothing[4] balm[5] of the ocean.

'We need to move again,' Tain is saying. 'But not uphill this time – there's not enough land left for us.'

Mara feels the panic lurch in her stomach. She grips Tain's hand.

'We need to find a new home in the world,' Tain declares. 'Soon, Mara, before it's too late.'

1 surge (n): *Welle* **2** barren: infertile **3** haven: safe area **4** soothing: *wohltuend* **5** balm: *Balsam*

Saci Lloyd
Carbon Rationing

Saci Lloyd was born in 1967 in Manchester but spent part of her childhood in Wales. After graduating from the University of Manchester, Lloyd spent some years working as a cartoonist and touring the USA in a band. She later returned to the United Kingdom and worked in the advertising as well as film and television industries. Lloyd now teaches media studies and design at a college in London. In addition to *The Carbon Diaries 2015*, from which the following extract is taken, and *The Carbon Diaries 2017*, Lloyd has published other science-fiction novels such as *Momentum* (2011), *Quantum Drop* (2013). *The End of the World as We Know It* (2015). In contrast to many other young adult dystopias, *The Carbon Diaries* series is often referred to as 'soft apocalypse' as it chronicles how societies changes as a result of global warming.

Each of us has a carbon footprint. If you wanted to reduce your carbon footprint, what measures would you take?

Thurs, Jan 1st

Exhausted. The whole family looks like death after an all-day meeting. The last time we were all in one place together for more than 3 hours was when my sister, Kim, locked us in a holiday cottage in France for the whole of Millennium night[1] by mistake. Happy times. Today she locked just herself in her bedroom and sulked[2] until Dad got her to come out. Typical. Mum is Being Very Positive – ranting about when she did voluntary work in the 80s on a kibbutz[3] in Israel, knitting lentil ponchos and *it being the best days of her life.*

1 Millenium night: the night when the year 2000 started **2** sulk: *schmollen*
3 kibbutz: collective community in Israel

Dad muttered[1] that we shouldn't just focus on it being difficult, but think up a New Year's wish list. He typed our answers into his laptop. Ever since he got made Head of Travel and Tourism at Greenham College he zaps everything into Excel and files it as evidence. Mum says The System's got him by the Balls.

Brown Family New Year's Luxury Item List. 01/01/15			
Nick Brown	Julia Brown	Laura Brown	Kim Brown
One hour of quiet time in study per evening	The car (Saab hydro-hybrid 9.50 Convertible[2])	Keep the dirty angels up and running	Her life back
Archers'[3] Omnibus[4] on Sundays	Shisheido face and body range	24/7 access to e-pod	
	Inner growth	Ravi Datti to notice me (did not write this down)	

She just rolled her eyes when she saw Dad's list. She said, 'God, Nick, I didn't know we were so *polarized*.'

Fri, Jan 2nd

My parents are in deep denial[5]; they've spent the day on the sofa, staring blindly at the TV like amoebas[6]. So far they've back-to-back watched *Dumbo, Mary Poppins* and *Judy Garland: a Tribute in Song*.

1 mutter: *murmeln* **2** convertible: *Cabrio* **3** Archers: popular radio soap opera **4** omnibus: programme that combines several recent episodes of a series **5** in denial: refusing to accept that sth. unpleasant is true **6** amoeba: *Amöbe*

I saw Kim for a total 5.2 seconds when I answered the front door to a pizza deliveryman. She stormed out of her room and snatched the pizza box off me with dead eyes before marching back into her room again. She's so using my parents' death state to get her boyfriend, Paul, round and blaze[1] in her room. I caught a real blast when she opened her door.

I wanted to watch the news and check out the countdown to rationing, but fat chance of that in this house of drugs and musicals, so I sneaked out next door but one to Kieran's. When I got there he was unblocking his kitchen sink – which is kind of funny because Kieran is a single, gay hairdresser in his 30s and if anyone should be wiped out on the sofa and drooling[2] over musicals after an all-nighter[3] it should be him, really. But that's why I love him. He's actually not predictable and ground down to dust, the *total opposite* of most adults. I reckon if he can get away with it then maybe I can too, when my time comes.

'Hold this,' he groaned, handing me a bit of sink before ducking his head under again and poking upward viciously with a coat hanger. The plumbing let out a totally brutal gurgle and evil gunk exploded out of the plughole. Kieran screamed, 'Oh Jesus!' and sprang backward, shards of meat and grease and carrots streaming down his face. Gross.

He dived under the power shower and stayed there for one long time, so I flicked on Channel 4 News. They've got this big countdown clock in the studio with massive Day-Glo carbon symbols instead of numbers on its face. It was kind of like kid's TV cept[4] it's so real. Messed up.

Anyway, today's symbol was about food miles. The presenter stood in front of a split video screen and waved his arm towards the left-side screen, where there was a South African farmer holding out a ripe mango. On the other side there was a farmer in Kent holding a wrinkled apple. Basically a 12,000-air-mile mango versus

1 blaze (sl): smoke cannabis **2** drool over sth.: *in etwas schwelgen*
3 all-nighter: act of going out partying all night **4** cept (infml): except

a 40-minutes-in-the-back-of-a-dirty-old-truck apple. The carbon maths is a no-brainer[1], but life is definitely going to be a lot less glamorous.

This 60% reduction is way over the top. We were supposed to get there by 2030, but after the Great Storm everything changed and it all became more hectic. Even so, why is the UK going first? I know we were hit the hardest in the storm – that was one messed-up time; houses literally ripped out of the ground, thousands of people homeless over the whole winter, no petrol for a month. I guess something really happened to people then. It was like everyone went *That's enough. Stop now.* Europe's going to follow – I mean, they've got to in the end – but right now it's like they're happy for someone else to do it first. So it looks like we're the stupid guinea-pig freaks, giving up everything while the rest sit back and watch.

11 p.m. In bed now. *Jeeesus,* Kieran's got himself in a real state over rationing.

'I'm all washed up. Finished,' he kept moaning. 'It's the hunter-gatherer[2], macho, sink-unblocker's world now. What'll become of a little skinny hairdresser guy like me?'

Kieran goes to the gym about six times a week, so I told him he had gorgeous pecs[3], which usually sorts him out.

'Yeah, yeah, but what's the use when there'll be no clubs, no weekenders in Ibiza, no chilled Laurent-Perrier, no Versace? A male hairdresser can't be taken seriously without a lifestyle!"

'Like you do any of that stuff, anyway,' I snorted. 'You're always moaning[4] about those scene queens.'

'I know, I know – but they're taking my right to choose away!'

I checked he wasn't being ironic, but his mouth was all drawn down like a little boy.

When I got home, my parents were asleep in front of the TV screen, every single light in the house was blazing and Kim was

1 no-brainer: sth. that is easy to accept **2** hunter-gatherer: *Jäger und Sammler*
3 pecs: *Brustmuskeln* **4** moan about sth.: complain loudly about sth.

in the bath with the stereo and her bedroom HD on. I don't know what's gonna happen to this family once rationing really kicks in.

Sat, Jan 3rd

Dad sat us all down again tonight and took us thru[1] a disgusting government online form to work out what our family CO allowance actually is. It's heavy. Basically we've got a carbon allowance of 200 Carbon Points per month to spend on travel, heat and food. All other stuff like clothes and technology and books have already got the Carbon Points built into the price, so say you wanna buy a PC but it's been shipped over from China and built using dirty fossil fuel then you're gonna pay a lot more for it in Euros – cos[2] you're paying for all the energy that's gone into making it.

At first they set up a free trading system so that if you were rich you could just buy up carbon in cash and live how you wanted – but after the riots last September the Gov backed down and changed the rules so that no one's allowed to buy more than 50 extra points a month.

And the worst thing is, on top of all this, me and Kim have to give up loads of our points for the family energy allowance, which leaves us some pathetic amount for travel, college, going out ... The car's gonna be cut way back, all of us get access to the PC, TV, HD, stereo for only 2 hours a day, heating is down to 16°C in the living room and 1 hour a day for the rest of the house, showers max 5 minutes, baths only at weekend. We've got to choose – hairdryer, toaster, microwave, smartphone, de-ioniser[3] (Mum), kettle, lights, PDA, e-pod, fridge or freezer and on and on. Flights are a real no-no and shopping, travelling and going out not much better. It's all kind of a *choice*.

I sat there and thought about my band, the *dirty angels.* We've just got back together after a break for *musical differences* after

1 thru (infml spelling): through **2** cos (infml): because **3** de-ioniser: *Luftreiniger*

Claire got heavily into hardcore Straight Edge. She was so militant. You couldn't even unwrap a Snickers around her without a lecture on skinny cocoa-bean farmers. Anyway, she blew it by getting back with her snotty[1] boyfriend *and* eating a bacon sandwich – all on the same day – and so we're together again and sounding *sooooo* good right now. It's my dream.

And all the time everyone was saying stuff like, *Well, I'm not selling the car, I worked hard for it, and, I just want to go on my gap year and get away from your selfish messed-up generation, and I insist that one of the daily TV-hours is spent watching a current affairs programme.*

Mon, Jan 5th

Carbon cards came today ...

They've got these little blocks down one side going from green to red and as you use up your year's ration they fade away one by one till you're down to the last red and then you're all alone, sobbing in

1 snotty: *pampig*

the dark. Kim won't unwrap her card, she says if she touches it then that's all her youth gone. I felt pretty shaky unwrapping mine, not that I really have a youth in my family. My sister's got it.

Tues, Jan 6th

The whole of London exploded tonight. It was all pretty normal round ours till about 9. Friends of my parents had come for supper. They were talking all the usual shite[1], then Marcia Hamilton, head of hardback non-fiction at Penguin, suddenly crawled under the table and started pawing at my dad's leg, like a little lost poodle, *yelping:* 'I can't cope!' Dad clutched his knife and fork really tight and tried to pretend it wasn't happening. Then Mum slammed her hand on the table and went: 'Damn right – let it out, Marcia!' before pouring half a bottle of wine down her throat. She turned to Phil Hamilton and said, 'Will you dance with me to the passing of an era?' *Phil Hamilton,* who is 5 foot 5, bald, with a woman's bottom and acne at 47 years of age!

I thought I was going to puke[2]. I got myself out on the street – and breathed deep. Please God, let me die before their genes kick-start in me.

Anyway, once I was there, a sudden movement caught my eye – and I turned to see Ravi Datta leaning against his front door. His family moved in next door a few months ago, he goes to the same college as me and is in my Design Tech class. And he is fully gorgeous. He was silhouetted by a street-lamp, smoking a totally illegal cigarette and staring up at the rockets[3] the Leaders were setting off over the estate. The lamp kept flickering on and off, lighting up his face and jet-black hair. And the best thing of all is he doesn't *know* he's fit[4]. And the worst thing of all is he makes me so nervous and I say stuuupid things when I'm around him like pointing at his smoke and saying, 'That's gonna kill you.' He turned and grinned: 'So?' before taking in a last vicious pull and flicking the butt into the

1 shite: nonsense **2** puke: vomit **3** rockets: fireworks **4** fit (infml): sexy

sky in a shower of sparks. Then he went back inside the house. He hardly ever says anything. It makes me mad when gorgeous people won't talk because boring people never shut up.

I hung out for a while, just looking up at the stars, and then suddenly a rocket fizzed right over me and smashed into Kieran's upstairs-flat window. Kieran stormed out on to his balcony and started screaming at the estate about them all being homophobic pigs and hunter-gatherers. Then the whole Leader family came out on to the estate balconies and started wolf-whistling him.

There are about a hundred Leaders, but never at the same time because they're always in and out of prison or young offenders[1]. The top dog Leader is Tracey because she's too smart to get put inside. Tracey Leader has got arms like tree trunks. She's got a tweety bird[2] tattoo on her collar bone and is dead scary. When she laughs she throws her head back and her gold tooth *glistens* but her brother, Karl Leader, is totally fit. I don't know how the rest of the Leaders look like a horror film. He has got Bambi eyelashes and a chiselled[3] jawbone.

Anyway it could have been really bad for Kieran, but Tracey was in gold-tooth mood and sent over her cousin, Desiree Leader, with a bottle of Cava to say sorry. And so me and Kieran wandered the streets, all the way to Blackheath, swigging from the bottle. Bringing in the new era in style. The roads were full of crazy people and there was smoke and explosions and screaming and singing and fights and madness everywhere.

I'm excited.

1 young offenders: (here) prison for teenagers **2** tweety bird: name of a cartoon character **3** chiselled: well-formed

James Tiptree, Jr.
The Girl Who Was Plugged in

James Tiptree, Jr. (1915–1987) was one of the pseudonyms used by the American writer and psychologist Alice B. Sheldon to publish most of her science-fiction short stories and novels between the 1960s and 1980s. Mainly due to her style, Tiptree has often been considered one of the best modern science-fiction authors. Tiptree was the first woman in many traditional male occupations: following her experience in intelligence work in the army, she later worked for the CIA. After graduating and writing her thesis in psychology, Tiptree focused on writing science-fiction stories like 'Birth of a Salesman' (1976) and 'The Last Flight of Dr. Ain' (1969). Many of her stories have become classics of the genre. Her novella *The Girl Who Was Plugged in* was published in 1974. The most remarkable fact about Tiptree's career is that she managed to hide her real identity for many years, always making sure that her age and gender remained secret. Tiptree ended her and her husband's lives when she was 72.

Imagine that in a future world there were no advertisements. Think of ways in which cooperations and companies might influence your decision to buy things.

Listen, zombie. Believe me. What I could tell you – you with your silly hands leaking[1] sweat on your growth-stocks portfolio[2]. One-ten lousy[3] hacks of AT&T on twenty-point margin and you think you're Evel Knievel[4]. AT&T? You doubleknit dummy, how I'd love to show you something.

Look, dead daddy, I'd say. See for instance that rotten girl?

1 leak sth. : *etwas austreten lassen* **2** growth-stocks portfolio: *Wachstumsaktien-paket* **3** lousy: very bad or poor **4** Evel Knievel: famous US stuntman

In the crowd over there, that one gaping[1] at her gods. One rotten girl in the city of the future. (That's what I said.) Watch.

She's jammed among bodies, craning and peering with her soul yearning[2] out of her eyeballs. Love! Oo-ooh, love them! Her gods are coming out of a store called Body East. Three young-bloods, larking[3] along loverly[4]. Dressed like simple street-people but ... smashing. See their great eyes swivel above their nose-filters, their hands lift shyly, their inhumanly tender lips melt? The crowd moans. Love! This whole boiling megacity, this whole fun future world loves its gods.

You don't believe gods, dad? Wait. Whatever turns you on, there's a god in the future for you, custom-made. Listen to this mob. 'I touched his foot. Ow-oow, I TOUCHED Him!'

Even the people in the GTX tower up there love the gods – in their own way and for their own reasons.

The funky girl on the street, she just loves. Grooving on their beautiful lives, their mysterioso problems. No one ever told her about mortals who love a god and end up as a tree or a sighing sound. In a million years it'd never occur to her that her gods might love her back.

She's squashed against the wall now as the godlings come by.

They move in a clear space. A holocam bobs above but its shadow never falls on them. The store display screens are magically clear of bodies as the gods glance in and a beggar underfoot is suddenly alone. They give him a token. 'Aaaaah!' goes the crowd.

Now one of them flashes some wild new kind of timer and they all trot to catch a shuttle, just like people. The shuttle stops for them – more magic. The crowd sighs, closing back. The gods are gone.

(In a room far from – but not unconnected to – the GTX tower a molecular[5] flipflop closes too, and three account tapes spin.)

1 gape: stare at sb./sth. with your mouth open because you are shocked or surprised **2** yearning out of her eyeballs: full of desire **3** lark: do sth. in a mischievous way **4** loverly (sl): in a lovely way **5** molecular (infml): fragmented or smaller part

Our girl is still stuck by the wall while guards and holocam equipment pull away. The adoration's[1] fading from her face. That's good, because now you can see she's the ugly of the world. A tall monument to pituitary dystrophy[2]. No surgeon would touch her. When she smiles, her jaw – it's half purple – almost bites her left eye out. She's also quite young, but who could care?

The crowd is pushing her along now, treating you to glimpses of her jumbled torso[3], her mismatched legs. At the corner she strains to send one last fond spasm after the godlings' shuttle. Then her face reverts to its usual expression of dim pain and she lurches onto the moving walkway, stumbling into people. The walkway junctions with another. She crosses, trips and collides with the casualty rail. Finally she comes out into a little place called a park. The sportshow is working, a basketball game in 3-di is going on right overhead. But all she does is squeeze onto a bench and huddle there while a ghostly free-throw goes by her ear.

After that nothing at all happens except a few furtive hand-mouth gestures which don't even interest her benchmates.

But you're curious about the city? So ordinary after all, in the FUTURE?

Ah, there's plenty to swing with here – and it's not all that far in the future, dad. But pass up the sci-fi stuff for now, like for instance the holovision technology that's put TV and radio in museums. Or the worldwide carrier field bouncing down from satellites, controlling communication and transport systems all over the globe. That was a spin-off from asteroid mining, pass it by. We're watching that girl.

I'll give you just one goodie. Maybe you noticed on the sportshow or the streets? No commercials. No ads.

That's right. NO ADS. An eyeballer for you.

Look around. Not a billboard, sign, slogan, jingle, skywrite, blurb, sublimflash, in this whole fun world. Brand names? Only in those

1 adoration: deep love and respect **2** pituitary dystrophy: a medical condition which causes weight gain and/or ugliness **3** torso: *Oberkörper*

ticky little peep-screens on the stores and you could hardly call that advertising. How does that finger you?

Think about it. That girl is still sitting there.

She's parked right under the base of the GTX tower as a matter of fact. Look way up and you can see the sparkles from the bubble on top, up there among the domes of godland. Inside that bubble is a boardroom. Neat bronze shield on the door: Global Transmissions Corporation – not that that means anything.

I happen to know there's six people in that room. Five of them technically male, and the sixth isn't easily thought of as a mother. They are absolutely unremarkable. Those faces were seen once at their nuptials[1] and will show again in their obituaries[2] and impress nobody either time. If you're looking for the secret Big Blue Meanies of the world, forget it. I know. Zen, do I know! Flesh? Power? Glory? You'd horrify them.

What they do like up there is to have things orderly, especially their communications. You could say they've dedicated their lives to that, to freeing the world from garble[3]. Their nightmares are about hemorrhages[4] of information: channels screwed up, plans misimplemented, garble creeping in. Their gigantic wealth only worries them, it keeps opening new vistas of disorder. Luxury? They wear what their tailors put on them, eat what their cooks serve them. See that old boy there – his name is Isham – he's sipping water and owning as he listens to a databall. The water was prescribed by his medistaff. It tastes awful. The databall also contains a disquieting message about his son, Paul.

But it's time to go back down, far below to our girl. Look! She's toppled over sprawling on the ground.

A tepid[5] commotion ensues among the bystanders. The consensus is she's dead, which she disproves by bubbling a little. And presently she's taken away by one of the superb ambulances

1 nuptials (pl; fml): wedding **2** obituary: a notice of death in a newspaper, with a short biography of the dead person **3** garble: transmission error resulting in a confusing message **4** hemorrhage (n): damaging loss of sth. **5** tepid: *lau*

of the future, which are a real improvement over ours when one happens to be around.

At the local bellevue[1] the usual things are done by the usual team of clowns aided by a saintly mop-pusher. Our girl revives enough to answer the questionnaire without which you can't die, even in the future. Finally she's cast up, a pumped-out hulk on a cot in the long, dim ward.

Again nothing happens for a while except that her eyes leak a little from the understandable disappointment of finding herself still alive.

But somewhere one GTX computer has been tickling another, and toward midnight something does happen. First comes an attendant who pulls screens around her. Then a man in a business doublet comes daintily down the ward. He motions the attendant to strip off the sheet and go.

The groggy girl-brute heaves up, big hands clutching at bodyparts you'd pay not to see.

'Burke? P. Burke, is that your name?'

'Y-yes.' Croak. 'Are you ... policeman?

'No. They'll be along shortly, I expect. Public suicide's a felony.'

'... I'm sorry.'

He has a 'corder[2] in his hand. 'No family, right?'

'No.'

'You're seventeen. One year city college. What did you study?'

'La-languages.'

'H'm. Say something.'

Unintelligible rasp[3].

He studies her. Seen close, he's not so elegant. Errand-boy type.

'Why did you try to kill yourself?'

She stares at him with dead-rat dignity, hauling up the gray sheet. Give him a point, he doesn't ask twice.

'Tell me, did you see Breath this afternoon?'

1 bellevue: (here) hospital **2** 'corder = recorder: *Aufnahmegerät* **3** rasp: *kratzendes Geräusch*

Dead as she nearly is, that ghastly[1] love-look wells up[2]. Breath is the three young gods, a loser's cult. Give the man another point, he interprets her expression.

'How would you like to meet them?'

The girl's eyes bug out grotesquely[3].

'I have a job for someone like you. It's hard work. If you did well you'd be meeting Breath and stars like that all the time.'

Is he insane? She's deciding she really did die.

'But it means you never see anybody you know again. Never, ever. You will be legally dead. Even the police won't know. Do you want to try?'

It all has to be repeated while her great jaw slowly sets. Show me the fire I walk through. Finally P. Burke's prints are in his 'corder, the man holding up the rancid girl-body without a sign of distaste. It makes you wonder what else he does.

And then – THE MAGIC. Sudden silent trot of litterbearers tucking P. Burke into something quite different from a bellevue stretcher[4], the oiled slide into the daddy of all luxury ambulances – real flowers in that holder! – and the long jarless rush to nowhere. Nowhere is warm and gleaming[5] and kind with nurses. (Where did you hear that money can't buy genuine kindness?) And clean clouds folding P. Burke into bewildered sleep.

... Sleep which merges into feedings and washings and more sleeps, into drowsy moments of afternoon where midnight should be, and gentle businesslike voices and friendly (but very few) faces, and endless painless hyposprays and peculiar[6] numbnesses. And later comes the steadying rhythm of days and nights, and a quickening which P. Burke doesn't identify as health, but only knows that the fungus place in her armpit is gone. And then she's up and following those few new faces with growing trust, first tottering, then walking strongly, all better now, clumping down the short hall to the tests, tests, tests, and the other things.

1 ghastly: unpleasant **2** well up: *aufwallen* **3** grotesque: ugly or distorted
4 stretcher: *Trage* **5** gleaming: bright and shiny **6** peculiar: strange

And here is our girl, looking –

If possible, worse than before. (You thought this was Cinderella transistorized?)

The disimprovement in her looks comes from the electrode jacks peeping out of her sparse hair, and there are other meldings of flesh and metal. On the other hand, that collar and spinal plate are really an asset; you won't miss seeing that neck.

P. Burke is ready for training in her new job.

The training takes place in her suite, and is exactly what you'd call a charm course. How to walk, sit, eat, speak, blow her nose, how to stumble, to urinate, to hiccup – DELICIOUSLY. How to make each nose-blow or shrug delightfully, subtly different from any ever spooled before. As the man said, it's hard work.

But P. Burke proves apt. Somewhere in that horrible body is a gazelle, a houri[1] who would have been buried forever without this crazy chance. See the ugly duckling go!

Only it isn't precisely P. Burke who's stepping, laughing, shaking out her shining hair. How could it be? P. Burke is doing it all right, but she's doing it through something. The something is to all appearances a live girl. (You were warned, this is the FUTURE.)

When they first open the big cryocase[2] and show her her new body she says just one word. Staring, gulping, 'How?'

Simple, really. Watch P. Burke in her sack and scuffs stump down the hall beside Joe, the man who supervises the technical part of her training. Joe doesn't mind P. Burke's looks, he hasn't noticed them. To Joe, system matrices are beautiful.

They go into a dim room containing a huge cabinet like a one-man sauna and a console for Joe. The room has a glass wall that's all dark now. And just for your information, the whole shebang[3] is five hundred feet underground near what used to be Carbondale, Pa[4].

Joe opens the sauna-cabinet like a big clamshell standing on end with a lot of funny business inside. Our girl shucks her shift and

1 houri: a beautiful young virgin **2** cryocase: a cold enclosure **3** the whole shebang (infml): the whole thing **4** Pa: Pennsylvania

walks into it bare, totally unembarrassed. Eager. She settles in face-forward, butting jacks into sockets. Joe closes it carefully onto her humpback. Clunk. She can't see in there or hear or move. She hates this minute. But how she loves what comes next!

Joe's at his console and the lights on the other side of the glass wall come up. A room is on the other side, all fluff and kicky bits, a girly bedroom. In the bed is a small mound of silk with a rope of yellow hair hanging out.

The sheets stirs and gets whammed back flat.

Sitting up in the bed is the darlingest girl child you've EVER seen. She quivers – porno for angels. She sticks both her little arms straight up, flips her hair, looks around full of sleepy pazazz[1]. Then she can't resist rubbing her hands down over her minibreasts and belly. Because, you see, it's the godawful P. Burke who is sitting there hugging her perfect girl-body, looking at you out of delighted eyes.

Then the kitten hops out of bed and crashes flat on the floor.

From the sauna in the dim room comes a strangled noise. P. Burke, trying to rub her wired-up elbow is suddenly smothered in two bodies, electrodes jerking in her flesh. Joe juggles inputs, crooning into his mike. The flurry passes; it's all right.

In the lighted room the elf gets up, casts a cute glare at the glass wall and goes into a transparent cubicle. A bathroom, what else? She's a live girl, and live girls have to go to the bathroom after a night's sleep even if their brains are in a sauna-cabinet in the next room. And P. Burke isn't in that cabinet, she's in the bathroom. Perfectly simple, if you have the glue for that closed training circuit that's letting her run her neural system by remote control.

Now let's get one thing clear. P. Burke does not feel her brain is in the sauna room, she feels she's in that sweet little body. When you wash your hands, do you feel the water is running on your brain? Of course not. You feel the water on your hand, although the 'feeling' is actually a potential-pattern flickering over the electrochemical jelly between your ears. And it's delivered there via the long circuits from

1 pazazz (infml): attractive combination of beautiful features

your hands. Just so, P. Burke's brain in the cabinet feels the water on her hands in the bathroom. The fact that the signals have jumped across space on the way in makes no difference at all. If you want the jargon, it's known as eccentric[1] projection or sensory reference and you've done it all your life. Clear?

Time to leave the honey-pot to her toilet training – she's made a booboo with the toothbrush, because P. Burke can't get used to what she sees in the mirror. But wait, you say. Where did that girl-body come from?

P. Burke asks that too, dragging out the words.

'They grow 'em,' Joe tells her. He couldn't care less about the flesh department. 'PDs. Placental decanters[2]. Modified embryos, see? Fit the control implants in later. Without a Remote Operator it's just a vegetable. Look at the feet – no callus[3] at all.' (He knows because they told him.)

'Oh ... oh, she's incredible ...'

'Yeah, a neat job. Want to try walking-talking mode today? You're coming on fast.'

And she is. Joe's reports and the reports from the nurse and the doctor and style man go to a bushy man upstairs who is some kind of medical cybertech but mostly a project administrator. His reports in turn go – to the GTX boardroom? Certainly not, did you think this is a big thing? His reports just go up. The point is, they're green, very green. P. Burke promises well.

So the bushy man – Doctor Tesla – has procedures to initiate. The little kitten's dossier in the Central Data Bank, for instance. Purely routine. And the phase-in schedule which will put her on the scene. This is simple: a small exposure in an off-network holoshow.

Next he has to line out the event which will fund and target her. That takes budget meetings, clearances, coordinations. The Burke project begins to recruit and grow. And there's the messy business

1 eccentric: unconventional and strange **2** placental decanter: a container to feed embryos artificially **3** callus: *Hornhaut*

of the name, which always gives Doctor Tesla an acute pain in the bush.

The name comes out weird, when it's suddenly discovered that Burke's 'P.' stands for 'Philadelphia', Philadelphia? The astrologer grooves on it. Joe thinks it would help identification. The semantics[1] girl references brotherly love, Liberty-Bell, main-line, low teratogenesis[2], blah-blah. Nicknames Philly? Pala? Pooty? Delphi? Is it good, bad? Finally 'Delphi' is gingerly declared goodo. ('Burke' is replaced by something nobody remembers.)

Coming along now. We're at the official checkout down in the underground suite, which is as far as the training circuits reach. The bushy Doctor Tesla is there, braced by two budgetary types and a quiet fatherly man whom he handles like hot plasma.

Joe swings the door wide and she steps shyly in.

Their little Delphi, fifteen and flawless.

Tesla introduces her around. She's child-solemn, a beautiful baby to whom something so wonderful has happened you can feel the tingles. She doesn't smile, she ... brims[3]. That brimming joy is all that shows of P. Burke, the forgotten hulk in the sauna next door. But P. Burke doesn't know she's alive – it's Delphi who lives, every warm inch of her.

One of the budget types lets go a libidinous[4] snuffle and freezes. The fatherly man, whose name is Mr. Cantle, clears his throat.

'Well, young lady, are you ready to go to work?'

'Yes sir,' gravely from the elf.

'We'll see. Has anybody told you what you're going to do for us?'

'No, sir.' Joe and Tesla exhale quietly.

'Good.' He eyes her, probing for the blind brain in the room next door.

'Do you know what advertising is?'

1 semantics: the meaning or different meanings of words or phrases **2** teratogenesis: the process by which malformations are produced in an embryo
3 brim: *übersprudeln vor Glück* **4** libidinous: more than normal sexual drive

He's talking dirty, hitting to shock. Delphi's eyes widen and her little chin goes up. Joe is in ecstasy[1] at the complex expressions P. Burke is getting through. Mr. Cantle waits.

'It's, well, it's when they used to tell people to buy things.' She swallows. 'It's not allowed.'

'That's right.' Mr. Cantle leans back, grave. 'Advertising as it used to be is against the law. A display other than the legitimate use of the product, intended to promote its sale. In former times every manufacturer was free to tout[2] his wares any way, place or time he could afford. All the media and most of the landscape was taken up with extravagant competing displays. The thing became uneconomic. The public rebelled. Since the so-called Huckster Act, sellers have been restrained to, I quote, displays in or on the product itself, visible during its legitimate use or in on-premise sales.' Mr. Cantle leans forward. 'Now tell me, Delphi, why do people buy one product rather than another?'

'Well ...' Enchanting puzzlement from Delphi. 'They, um, they see them and like them, or they hear about them from somebody?' (Touch of P. Burke there; she didn't say, from a friend.)

'Partly. Why did you buy your particular body-lift?'

'I never had a body-lift, sir.'

Mr. Cantle frowns; what gutters do they drag for these Remotes? 'Well, what brand of water do you drink?'

'Just what was in the faucet[3], sir,' says Delphi humbly. 'I – I did try to boil it –'

'Good God." He scowls; Tesla stiffens. 'Well, what did you boil it in? A cooker?'

The shining yellow head nods.

'What brand of cooker did you buy?'

'I didn't buy it, sir,' says frightened P. Burke through Delphi's lips. 'But – I know the best kind! Ananga has a Burnbabi, I saw the name when she –'

1 ecstasy: feeling of great happiness **2** tout [taʊt] sth.: try to persuade people to buy sth. **3** faucet (AE): *Wasserhahn*

'Exactly!" Cantle's fatherly beam comes back strong; the Burnbabi account is a strong one, too. 'You saw Ananga using one so you thought it must be good, eh? And it is good or a great human being like Ananga wouldn't be using it. Absolutely right. And now, Delphi, you know what you're going to be doing for us. You're going to show some products. Doesn't sound very hard, does it?'

'Oh, no, sir …' Baffled child's stare; Joe gloats.

'And you must never, never tell anyone what you're doing.' Cantle's eyes bore for the brain behind this seductive child.

'You're wondering why we ask you to do this, naturally. There's a very serious reason. All those products people use, foods and healthaids and cookers and cleaners and clothes and car – they're all made by people. Somebody put in years of hard work designing and making them. A man comes up with a fine new idea for a better product. He has to get a factory and machinery, and hire workmen. Now. What happens if people have no way of hearing about his product? Word-of-mouth is far too slow and unreliable. Nobody might ever stumble onto his new product or find out how good it was, right? And then he and all the people who worked for him – they'd go bankrupt, right? So, Delphi, there has to be some way that large numbers of people can get a look at a good new product, right? How? By letting people see you using it. You're giving that man a chance.'

Delphi's little head is nodding in happy relief.

'Yes, sir, I do see now – but sir, it seems so sensible, why don't they let you –'

Cantle smiles sadly.

'It's an overreaction, my dear. History goes by swings. People overreact and pass harsh unrealistic laws which attempt to stamp out an essential social process. When this happens, the people who understand have to carry on as best they can until the pendulum swings back.' He sighs. 'The Huckster Laws are bad, inhuman laws, Delphi, despite their good intent. If they were strictly observed they would wreak havoc[1]. Our economy, our society would be cruelly destroyed. We'd be back in caves!' His inner fire is showing; if the Huckster Laws were strictly enforced he'd be back punching a databank.

'It's our duty, Delphi. Our solemn social duty. We are not breaking the law. You will be using the product. But people wouldn't understand, if they knew. They would become upset, just as you did. So you must be very, very careful not to mention any of this to anybody.'

(And somebody will be very, very carefully monitoring Delphi's speech circuits.)

'Now we're all straight[2], aren't we? Little Delphi here' – He is speaking to the invisible creature next door – 'Little Delphi is going to live a wonderful, exciting life. She's going to be a girl people watch. And she's going to be using fine products people will be glad to know about and helping the good people who make them. Yours will be a genuine social contribution.' He keys up his pitch; the creature in there must be older.

Delphi digests this with ravishing gravity.

'But sir, how do I –?'

'Don't worry about a thing. You'll have people behind you whose job it is to select the most worthy products for you to use. Your job is just to do as they say. They'll show you what outfits to wear to parties, what suncars and viewers to buy and so on. That's all you have to do.'

Parties – clothes – suncars! Delphi's pink mouth opens. In P. Burke's starved seventeen-year-old head the ethics[3] of product sponsorship float far away.

'Now tell me in your own words what your job is, Delphi.'

'Yes sir. I – I'm to go to parties and buy things and use them as they tell me, to help the people who work in factories.'

'And what did I say was so important?'

1 wreak havoc: cause chaos **2** straight: clear about the situation **3** ethics (pl): philosophy of what is good and bad

'Oh – I shouldn't let anybody know, about the things.'

'Right.' Mr. Cantle has another paragraph he uses when the subject shows, well, immaturity. But he can sense only eagerness[1] here. Good. He doesn't really enjoy the other speech.

'It's a lucky girl who can have all the fun she wants while doing good for others, isn't it?' He beams around. There's a prompt[2] shuffling of chairs. Clearly this one is go.

Joe leads her out, grinning. The poor fool thinks they're admiring her coordination.

It's out into the world for Delphi now, and at this point the up-channels get used. On the administrative side account schedules are opened, subprojects activated. On the technical side the reserved bandwidth is cleared. (That carrier field, remember?) A new name is waiting for Delphi, a name she'll never hear. It's a long string of binaries which have been quietly cycling in a GTX tank ever since a certain Beautiful Person didn't wake up.

The name winks out of cycle, dances from pulses into modulations of modulations, whizzes through phasing, and shoots into a giga-band beam racing up to a synchronous[3] satellite poised over Guatemala. From there the beam pours twenty thousand miles back to earth again, forming an all-pervasive field of structured energies supplying tuned demand-points all over the CanAm quadrant.

With that field, if you have the right credit rating you can sit at a GTX console and operate a tuned ore-extractor[4] in Brazil. Or – if you have some simple credentials like being able to walk on water – you could shoot a spool into the network holocam shows running day and night in every home and dorm and rec. site. Or you could create a continent-wide traffic jam. Is it any wonder GTX guards those inputs like a sacred trust?

Delphi's 'name' appears as a tiny analyzable nonredundancy in the flux, and she'd be very proud if she knew about it. It would strike

1 eagerness: *Begeisterung* **2** prompt (adj): sudden **3** synchronous: (here) that orbits the earth **4** ore-extractor: machine that mines for minerals

P. Burke as magic; P. Burke never even understood robotcars. But Delphi is in no sense a robot. Call her a waldo[1] if you must. The fact is she's just a girl, a real live girl with her brain in an unusual place. A simple real-time on-line system with plenty of bit-rate – even as you and you.

The point of all this hardware, which isn't very much hardware in this society, is so Delphi can walk out of that underground suite, a mobile demand-point draining an omnipresent fieldform. And she does – eighty-nine pounds of tender girl flesh and blood with a few metallic components, stepping out into the sunlight to be taken to her new life. A girl with everything going for her including a meditech escort. Walking lovely, stopping to widen her eyes at the big antennae system overhead.

The mere fact that something called P. Burke is left behind down underground has no bearing at all. P. Burke is totally un-self aware and happy as a clam in its shell. (Her bed has been moved into the waldo cabinet room now.) And P. Burke isn't in the cabinet; P. Burke is climbing out of an airvan in a fabulous Colorado beef preserve and her name is Delphi. Delphi is looking at live Charolais steers[2] and live cottonwoods and aspens[3] gold against the blue smog and stepping over live grass to be welcomed by the reserve super's wife.

The super's wife is looking forward to a visit from Delphi and her friends and by a happy coincidence there's a holocam outfit here doing a piece for the nature nuts.

You could write the script yourself now, while Delphi learns a few rules about structural interferences and how to handle the tiny time lag which results from the new forty-thousand-mile parenthesis[4] in her nervous system. That's right – the people with the leased holocam rig naturally find the gold aspen shadows look a lot better on Delphi's flank than they do on a steer. And Delphi's face improves the mountains too, when you can see them. But the nature freaks aren't quite as joyful as you'd expect.

1 waldo: person who controls an object remotely **2** Charolais steer: type of cow
3 cottonwood, aspen: types of tree **4** parenthesis: interval

'See you in Barcelona, kitten,' the head man says sourly as they pack up.

'Barcelona?' echoes Delphi with that charming little subliminal lag. She sees where his hand is and steps back.

'Cool, it's not her fault,' another man says wearily. He knocks back his grizzled hair. 'Maybe they'll leave in some of the gut.'

Delphi watches them go off to load the spools on the GTX transport for processing. Her hand roves over the breast the man had touched. Back under Carbondale, P. Burke has discovered something new about her Delphi-body.

About the difference between Delphi and her own grim carcass.

She's always known Delphi has almost no sense of taste or smell. They explained about that: only so much bandwidth. You don't have to taste a suncar, do you? And the slight overall dimness of Delphi's sense of touch – she's familiar with that, too. Fabrics that would prickle P. Burke's own hide feel like a cool plastic film to Delphi.

But the blank spots. It took her a while to notice them. Delphi doesn't have much privacy; investments of her size don't. So she's slow about discovering there's certain definite places where her beastly P. Burke body feels things that Delphi's dainty flesh does not. H'mm! Channel space again, she thinks – and forgets it in the pure bliss of being Delphi.

You ask how a girl could forget a thing like that? Look. P. Burke is about as far as you can get from the concept girl. She's a female, yes – but for her, sex is a four-letter word spelled P-A-I-N. She isn't quite a virgin. You don't want the details; she'd been about twelve and the freak-lovers were bombed blind. When they came down they threw her out with a small hole in her anatomy and a mortal one elsewhere. She dragged off to buy her first and last shot and she can still hear the clerk's incredulous guffaws.

Do you see why Delphi grins, stretching her delicious little numb body in the sun she faintly feels? Beams, saying, 'Please, I'm ready now.'

Ready for what? For Barcelona like the sour man said, where his nature-thing is now making it strong in the amateur section of the

Festival. A winner! Like he also said, a lot of strip-mines and dead fish have been scrubbed but who cares with Delphi's darling face so visible?

So it's time for Delphi's face and her other delectabilities to show on Barcelona's Playa Neuva. Which means switching her channel to the EurAf synchsat.

They ship her at night so the nanosecond transfer isn't even noticed by that insignificant part of Delphi that lives five hundred feet under Carbondale, so excited the nurse has to make sure she eats. The circuit switches while Delphi 'sleeps', that is, while P. Burke is out of the waldo cabinet. The next time she plugs in to open Delphi's eyes it's no different – do you notice which relay boards your phone calls go through?

And now for the event that turns the sugarcube from Colorado into the PRINCESS.

Literally true, he's a prince, or rather an Infante of an old Spanish line that got shined up in the Neomonarchy[1]. He's also eighty-one, with a passion for birds – the kind you see in zoos. Now it suddenly turns out that he isn't poor at all. Quite the reverse; his old sister laughs in their tax lawyer's face and starts restoring the family hacienda[2] while the Infante totters out to court Delphi. And little Delphi begins to live the life of the gods.

What do gods do? Well, everything beautiful. But (remember Mr. Cantle?) the main point is Things. Ever see a god empty-handed? You can't be a god without at least a magic girdle or an eight-legged horse. But in the old days some stone tablets or winged sandals or a chariot drawn by virgins would do a god for life. No more! Gods make it on novelty now. By Delphi's time the hunt for new god-gear is turning the earth and seas inside-out and sending frantic fingers to the stars. And what gods have, mortals desire.

So Delphi starts on a Euromarket shopping spree squired by her old Infante, thereby doing her bit to stave off social collapse.

1 Neomonarchy: new monarchy **2** hacienda: large estates usu. in Spanish-speaking countries

Social what? Didn't you get it, when Mr. Cantle talked about a world where advertising is banned and fifteen billion consumers are glued to their holocam shows? One capricious[1] self-powered god can wreck you.

Take the nose-filter massacre. Years, the industry sweated years to achieve an almost invisible enzymatic filter. So one day a couple of pop-gods show up wearing nose-filters like big purple bats. By the end of the week the world market is screaming for purple bats. Then it switched to bird-heads and skulls, but by the time the industry retooled the crazies had dropped bird-heads and gone to injection globes. Blood!

Multiply that by a million consumer industries and you can see why it's economic to have a few controllable goods. Especially with the beautiful hunk of space R&D the Peace Department laid out for, and which the taxpayers are only too glad to have taken off their hands by an outfit like GTX which everybody knows is almost a public trust.

And so you – or rather, GTX – find a creature like P. Burke and give her Delphi. And Delphi helps keep things orderly, she does what you tell her to. Why? That's right, Mr. Cantle never finished his speech.

But here come the tests of Delphi's button-nose twinkling in the torrent of news and entertainment. And she's noticed. The feedback shows a flock[2] of viewers turning up the amps when this country baby gets tangled in her new colloidal body-jewels. She registers at a couple of major scenes, too, and when the Infante gives her a suncar, little Delphi trying out suncars is a tiger. There's a solid response in high-credit country. Mr. Cantle is humming his happy tune as he cancels a Benelux subnet option to guest her on a nude cook-show called Work Venus.

And now for the superposh old-world wedding! The hacienda has Moorish baths and six-foot silver candelabra[3] and real black horses

1 capricious: quick to change moods **2** flock: a large group of people **3** candelabra: holder for several candles or lamps

and the Spanish Vatican blesses them. The final event is a grand gaucho ball with the old prince and his little Infanta on a bowered balcony. She's a spectacular doll of silver lace, wildly launching toy doves at her new friends whirling by below.

The Infante beams, twitches his old nose to the scent of her sweet excitement. His doctor has been very helpful. Surely now, after he has been so patient with the suncars and all the nonsense –

The child looks up at him, saying something incomprehensible about 'breath'. He makes out that she's complaining about the three singers she had begged for.

'They've changed!' she marvels. 'Haven't they changed? They're so dreary. I'm so happy now!'

And Delphi falls fainting against a gothic vargueno[1].

Her American duenna[2] rushes up, calls help. Delphi's eyes are open, but Delphi isn't there. The duenna pokes among Delphi's hair, slaps her. The old prince grimaces. He has no idea what she is beyond an excellent solution to his tax problems, but he had been a falconer[3] in his youth. There comes to his mind the small pinioned birds which were flung up to stimulate the hawks. He pockets the veined claw to which he had promised certain indulgences and departs to design his new aviary.

And Delphi also departs with her retinue to the Infante's newly discovered yacht. The trouble isn't serious. It's only that five thousand miles away and five hundred feet down P. Burke has been doing it too well.

They've always known she has terrific aptitude[4]. Joe says he never saw a Remote take over so fast. No disorientations, no rejections. The psychomed talks about self-alienation. She's going into Delphi like a salmon to the sea.

1 vargueno: portable desk **2** duenna: elderly woman who looks after a younger woman **3** falconer: a person who trains birds of prey **4** aptitude: a natural ability to do something

She isn't eating or sleeping, they can't keep her out of the body-cabinet to get her blood moving, there are necroses[1] under her grisly sit-down. Crisis!

So Delphi gets a long 'sleep' on the yacht and P. Burke gets it pounded through her perforated[2] head that she's endangering Delphi. (Nurse Fleming thinks of that, thus alienating the psychomed.)

They rig a pool down there (Nurse Fleming again) and chase P. Burke back and forth. And she loves it. So naturally when they let her plug in again Delphi loves it too. Every noon beside the yacht's hydrofoils darling Delphi clips along in the blue sea they've warned her not to drink. And every night around the shoulder of the world an ill-shaped thing in a dark burrow beats its way across a sterile pool.

So presently the yacht stands up on its foils and carries Delphi to the program Mr. Cantle has waiting. It's long-range; she's scheduled for at least two decades' product life. Phase One calls for her to connect with a flock of young ultra-riches who are romping loose between Brioni[3] and Djakarta[4] where a competitor named PEV could pick them off.

A routine luxgear op, see; no politics, no policy angles, and the main budget items are the title and the yacht which was idle anyway. The storyline is that Delphi goes to accept some rare birds for her prince – who cares? The point is that the Haiti area is no longer radioactive and look! – the gods are there. And so are several new Carib West Happy Isles which can afford GTX rates, in fact two of them are GTX subsids.

But you don't want to get the idea that all these newsworthy people are wired-up robbies, for pity's sake. You don't need many if they're placed right. Delphi asks Joe about that when he comes

1 necrosis: death of part of your body because it lacks blood **2** perforated: having small holes **3** Brioni: island in Croatia **4** Djakarta = Jakarta: capital of Indonesia

down to Baranquilla to check her over. (P. Burke's own mouth hasn't said much for a while.)

'Are there many like me?'

'Nobody's like you, buttons. Look, are you still getting that Van Allen warble?'

'I mean, like Davy. Is he a Remote?'

(Davy is the lad who is helping her collect the birds. A sincere redhead who needs a little more exposure.)

'Davy? He's one of Mart's boys, some psychojob. They haven't any channel.'

'What about the real ones? Djuma van O, or Ali, or Jim Ten?'

'Djuma was born with a pile of GTX basic where her brain should be, she's nothing but a pain. Jimsy does what his astrologer[1] tells him. Look, peanut, where do you get the idea you aren't real? You're the reallest. Aren't you having joy?'

'Oh, Joe!' Flinging her little arms around him and his analyzer grids. 'Oh, me gusto mucho, muchissimo!'

'Hey, hey.' He pets her yellow head, folding the analyzer.

Three thousand miles north and five hundred feet down a forgotten hulk in a body-waldo glows.

And is she having joy. To waken out of the nightmare of being P. Burke and find herself a peri, a star-girl? On a yacht in paradise with no more to do than adorn herself and play with toys and attend revels and greet her friends – her, P. Burke, having friends! – and turn the right way for the holocams? Joy!

And it shows. One look at Delphi and the viewers know: DREAMS CAN COME TRUE.

Look at her riding pillions on Davy's sea-bike, carrying an apoplectic[2] macaw[3] in a silver hoop. Oh, Morton, let's go there this winter! Or learning the Japanese chinchona from that Kobe group, in a dress that looks like a blowtorch rising from one knee,

1 astrologer: a person that uses the stars to predict the future **2** apoplectic: very angry **3** macaw: type of parrot

and which should sell big in Texas. Morton, is that real fire? Happy, happy little girl!

And Davy. He's her pet and her baby and she loves to help him fix his red-gold hair. (P. Burke marveling[1], running Delphi's fingers through the curls.) Of course Davy is one of Matt's boys – not impotent[2] exactly, but very very low drive. (Nobody knows exactly what Matt does with his bitty budget but the boys are useful and one or two have made names.) He's perfect for Delphi; in fact the psychomed lets her take him to bed, two kittens in a basket. Davy doesn't mind the fact that Delphi 'sleeps' like the dead. That's when P. Burke is out of the body-waldo up at Carbondale, attending to her own depressing needs.

A funny thing about that. Most of her sleepy-time Delphi's just a gently ticking lush little vegetable waiting for P. Burke to get back on the controls. But now and again Delphi all by herself smiles a bit or stirs in her 'sleep'. Once she breathed a sound: 'Yes.'

Under Carbondale, P. Burke knows nothing. She's asleep too, dreaming of Delphi, what else? But if the bushy Dr. Tesla had heard that single syllable his bush would have turned snow-white. Because Delphi is TURNED OFF.

He doesn't. Davy is too dim to notice and Delphi's staff boss, Hopkins wasn't monitoring.

And they've all got something else to think about now, because the cold-fire dress sells half a million copies, and not only in Texas. The GTX computers already know it. When they correlate a minor demand for macaws in Alaska the problem comes to human attention: Delphi is something special.

It's a problem, see, because Delphi is targeted on a limited consumer bracket. Now it turns out she has mass-pop potential – those macaws in Fairbanks, man! – it's like trying to shoot mice with an ABM[3]. A whole new ball game. Dr. Tesla and the fatherly Mr. Cantle start going around in headquarters circles and buddy-

1 marvel: be filled with wonder **2** impotent: unable to have sex **3** ABM: anti-ballistic missile

lunching together when they can get away from a seventh-level weasel boy who scares them both.

In the end it's decided to ship Delphi down to the GTX holocam enclave in Chile to try a spot on one of the mainstream shows. (Never mind why an Infanta takes up acting.) The holocam complex occupies a couple of mountains where an observatory once used the clear air. Holocam total-environment shells are very expensive and electronically super-stable. Inside them actors can move freely without going off- register and the whole scene or any selected part will show up in the viewer's home in complete 3-di, so real you can look up their noses and much denser than you get from mobile rigs. You can blow a tit ten feet tall when there's no molecular skiffle around. The enclave looks – well, take everything you know about Hollywood-Burbank and throw it away. What Delphi sees coming down is a neat giant mushroom-farm, domes of all sizes up to monsters for the big games and stuff. It's orderly. The idea that art thrives on creative flamboyance[1] has long been torpedoed by proof that what art needs is computers. Because this showbiz has something TV and Hollywood never had – automated inbuilt viewer feedback. Samples, ratings, critics, polls? Forget it. With that carrier field you can get real-time response-sensor readouts from every receiver in the world, served up at your console. That started as a thingie to give the public more influence on content.

Yes.

Try it, man. You're at the console. Slice to the sex-age-educ-econ-ethno-cetera audience of your choice and start. You can't miss. Where the feedback warms up, give 'em more of that. Warm – warmer – hot! You've hit it – the secret itch under those hides, the dream in those hearts. You don't need to know its name. With your hand controlling all the input and your eye reading all the response you can make them a god ... and somebody'll do the same for you.

1 flamboyance: the quality being different, confident and exciting in a way that attracts attention

But Delphi just sees rainbows, when she gets through the degaussing[1] ports and the field relay and takes her first look at the insides of those shells. The next thing she sees is a team of shapers and technicians descending on her, and millisecond timers everywhere. The tropical leisure is finished. She's in gigabuck mainstream now, at the funnel maw of the unceasing hose that's pumping the sight and sound and flesh and blood and sobs and laughs and dreams of reality into the world's happy head. Little Delphi is going plonk into a zillion homes in prime time and nothing is left to chance. Work!

And again Delphi proves apt. Of course it's really P. Burke down under Carbondale who's doing it, but who remembers that carcass? Certainly not P. Burke, she hasn't spoken through her own mouth for months. Delphi doesn't even recall dreaming of her when she wakes up.

As for the show itself, don't bother. It's gone on so long no living soul could unscramble the plotline. Delphi's trial spot has something to do with a widow and her dead husband's brother's amnesia[2].

The flap comes after Delphi's spots begin to flash out along the world-hose and the feedback appears. You've guessed it, of course. Sensational! As you'd say, they IDENTIFY.

The report actually says something like InsldnEmp with a string of percentages meaning that Delphi not only has it for anybody with a Y-chromosome, but also for women and everything in between. It's the sweet supernatural jackpot, the million- to-one.

Remember your Harlow[3]? A sexpot, sure. But why did bitter hausfraus in Gary and Memphis know that the vanilla-ice-cream goddess with the white hair and crazy eyebrows was their baby girl? And write loving letters to Jean warning her that their husbands weren't good enough for her? Why? The GTX analysts don't know either, but they know what to do with it when it happens.

(Back in his bird sanctuary the old Infante spots it without benefit of computers and gazes thoughtfully at his bride in widow's

1 degauss: remove unwanted magnetism to make an image clearer on a monitor
2 amnesia: total or partial loss of memory **3** Jean Harlow: US actress in 1930s

weeds. It might, he feels, be well to accelerate the completion of his studies.)

The excitement reaches down to the burrow under Carbondale where P. Burke gets two medical exams in a week and a chronically inflamed electrode is replaced. Nurse Fleming also gets an assistant who doesn't do much nursing but is very interested in access doors and identity tabs.

And in Chile little Delphi is promoted to a new home up among the stars' residential spreads and a private jitney to carry her to work. For Hopkins there's a new computer terminal and a full-time schedule man. What is the schedule crowded with?

Things.

And here begins the trouble. You probably saw that coming too.

'What does she think she is, a goddam consumer rep?' Mr. Cantle's fatherly face in Carbondale contorts.

'The girl's upset,' Miss Fleming says stubbornly. 'She believes that, what you told her about helping people and good new products.'

'They are good products,' Mr. Cantle snaps automatically, but his anger is under control. He hasn't got where he is by irrelevant reactions.

'She says the plastic gave her a rash and the glo-pills made her dizzy.'

'Good god, she shouldn't swallow them,' Doctor Tesla puts in agitatedly.

'You told her she'd use them,' persists[1] Miss Fleming. Mr. Cantle is busy figuring how to ease this problem to the weasel-faced young man. What, was it a goose that lays golden eggs?

Whatever he says to level Seven, down in Chile the offending products vanish. And a symbol goes into Delphi's tank matrix, one that means roughly Balance unit resistance against PR index. This means that Delphi's complaints will be endured as long as her Pop Response stays above a certain level. (What happens when it sinks need not concern us.) And to compensate, the price of her exposure-

1 persist: continue to insist on sth

time rises again. She's a regular on the show now and response is still climbing.

See her under the sizzling lasers, in a holocam shell set up as a walkway accident. (The show is guesting an acupuncture school expert.)

'I don't think this new body-life is safe,' Delphi's saying. 'It's made a funny blue spot on me – look, Mr. Vere.'

She wiggles to show where the mini-gray pak that imparts a delicious sense of weightlessness is attached.

'So don't leave it on, Dee. With your meat – watch that deck-spot, it's starting to synch.'

'But if I don't wear it it isn't honest. They should insulate it more or something, don't you see?'

The show's beloved old father, who is the casualty, gives a senile snigger.

'I'll tell them,' Mr. Vere mutters. 'Look now, as you step back bend like this so it just shows, see? And hold two beats.'

Obediently[1] Delphi turns, and through the dazzle her eyes connect with a pair of strange dark ones. She squints. A quite young man is lounging alone by the port, apparently waiting to use the chamber.

Delphi's used by now to young men looking at her with many peculiar expressions, but she isn't used to what she gets here. A jolt of something somber and knowing. Secrets.

'Eyes! Eyes, Dee!'

She moves through the routine, stealing peeks at the stranger. He stares back. He knows something.

When they let her go she comes shyly to him.

'Living wild, kitten.' Cool voice, hot underneath.

'What do you mean?'

'Dumping on the product. You trying to get dead?'

'But it isn't right,' she tells him. 'They don't know, but I do, I've been wearing it.'

1 obedient: willing to follow orders

His cool is jolted.

'You're out of your head.'

'Oh, they'll see I'm right when they check it,' she explains. 'They're just so busy. When I tell them –'

He is staring down at little flower-face. His mouth opens, closes. 'What are you doing in this sewer anyway? Who are you?'

Bewilderedly[1] she says, 'I'm Delphi.'

'Holy Zen.'

'What's wrong. Who are you, please?'

Her people are moving her out now, nodding at him.

'Sorry we, ran over, Mister Uhunh,' the script girl says.

He mutters[2] something but it's lost as her convoy[3] bustles her toward the flower-decked jitney[4].

(Hear the click of an invisible ignition-train being armed?)

'Who was he?' Delphi asks her hair man.

The hair man is bending up and down from his knees as he works.

'Paul. Isham. Three,' he says and puts a comb in his mouth.

'Who's that? I can't see.'

He mumbles around the comb, meaning 'Are you jiving[5]?' Because she has to be, in the middle of the GTX enclave.

Next day there's a darkly smoldering[6] face under a turban-towel when Delphi and the show's paraplegic[7] go to use the carbonated pool.

She looks.

He looks.

And the next day, too.

(Hear that automatic sequencer[8] cutting in? The system couples, the fuels begin to travel.)

1 bewildered: confused **2** mutter: say sth. in a low voice to yourself **3** convoy: (here) a group of people in a team **4** jitney: a vehicle carrying passengers **5** jive: (here) joke **6** smoldering (AE spelling): showing anger or other powerful emotions **7** paraplegic: person who has lost the ability to use their lower body **8** sequencer: a device storing orders with specific set actions

Poor old Isham senior. You have to feel sorry for a man who values order: when he begets young, genetic information is still transmitted[1] in the old ape way. One minute it's a happy midget with a rubber duck – look around and here's this huge healthy stranger, opaquely emotional, running with God knows who. Questions are heard where there's nothing to question, and eruptions claiming to be moral outrage. When this is called to Papa's attention – it may take time, in that boardroom – Papa does what he can, but without immortality-juice the problem is worrisome.

And young Paul Isham is a bear. He's bright and articulate and tender-souled and incessantly[2] active and he and his friends are choking with appallment[3] at the world their fathers made. And it hasn't taken Paul long to discover that his father's house has many mansions and even the GTX computers can't relate everything to everything else. He noses out a decaying project which adds up to something like Sponsoring Marginal Creativity (the free-lance team that 'discovered' Delphi was one such grantee[4]). And from there it turns out that an agile lad named Isham can get his hands on a viable packet of GTX holocam facilities.

So here he is with his little band, way down the mushroom-farm mountain, busily spooling a show which has no relation to Delphi's. It's built on bizarre techniques and unsettling distortions[5] pregnant[6] with social protest. An underground expression to you.

All this isn't unknown to his father, of course, but so far it has done nothing more than deepen Isham senior's apprehensive frown.

Until Paul connects with Delphi.

And by the time Papa learns this, those invisible hypergolics have exploded, the energy-shells are rushing out. For Paul, you see, is the genuine article. He's serious. He dreams. He even reads – for

1 transmit sth: pass sth. (e.g. information) to sth. else **2** incessant: continuing without interruption **3** apallment: *Entsetzen* **4** grantee: *Zuwendungs-empfänger* **5** distortion: *Verzerrung* **6** pregnant with sth.: filled with sth.

example, *Green Mansions*[1] – and he wept fiercely when those fiends burned Rima alive.

When he hears that some new GTX pussy is making it big he sneers and forgets it. He's busy. He never connects the name with this little girl making her idiotic, doomed protest in the holocam chamber. This strangely simple little girl.

And she comes and looks up at him and he sees Rima, lost Rima the enchanted bird girl, and his unwired human heart goes twang.

And Rima turns out to be Delphi.

Do you need a map? The angry puzzlement. The rejection of the dissonance[2] Rima-hustling-for-GTX-My-Father. Garbage, cannot be. The loitering[3] around the pool to confirm the swindle ... dark eyes hitting on blue wonder, jerky words exchanged in a peculiar stillness ... the dreadful reorganization of the image into Rima-Delphi in my Father's tentacles—

You don't need a map.

Nor for Delphi either, the girl who loved her gods. She's seen their divine flesh close now, heard their unamplified voices call her name. She's played their god-games, worn their garlands. She's even become a goddess herself, though she doesn't believe it. She's not disenchanted, don't think that. She's still full of love. It's just that some crazy kind of hope hasn't –

Really you can skip all this, when the loving little girl on the yellow-brick road meets a Man. A real human male burning with angry compassion[4] and grandly concerned with human justice, who reaches for her with real male arms and – boom! She loves him back with all her heart.

A happy trip, see?

Except.

1 Green Mansions: novel (1904) set in the Amazon jungle about a mysterious young girl called Rima **2** dissonance: lack of agreement between two things **3** loiterering: standing or waiting around with no purpose **4** compassion: feeling of sympathy for sb.

Except that it's really P. Burke five thousand miles away who loves Paul. P. Burke the monster, down in a dungeon, smelling of electrode-paste. A caricature of a woman burning, melting, obsessed with true love. Trying over twenty-double-thousand miles of hard vacuum to reach her beloved through the girl-flesh numbed by an invisible film. Feeling his arms around the body he thinks is hers, fighting through shadows to give herself to him. Trying to taste and smell him through beautiful dead nostrils, to love him back with a body that goes dead in the heart of the fire.

Perhaps you get P. Burke's state of mind?

She has phases. The trying, first. And the shame. The SHAME. I am not what thou lovest. And the fiercer trying. And the realization that there is no, no way, none. Never. Never. ... A bit delayed, isn't it, her understanding that the bargain she made was forever? P. Burke should have noticed those stories about mortals who end up as grasshoppers.

You see the outcome – the funneling of all this agony into one dumb protoplasmic drive to fuse with Delphi. To leave, to close out the beast she is chained to. To become Delphi.

Of course it's impossible.

However her torments have an effect on Paul. Delphi-as-Rima is a potent enough love object, and liberating Delphi's mind requires hours of deeply satisfying instruction in the rottenness of it all. Add in Delphi's body worshipping his flesh, burning in the fire of P. Burke's savage heart – do you wonder Paul is involved?

That's not all.

By now they're spending every spare moment together and some that aren't so spare.

'Mister Isham, would you mind staying out of this sports sequence? The script calls for Davy here.'

(Davy's still around, the exposure did him good.)

'What's the difference?' Paul yawns. 'It's just an ad. I'm not blocking that thing.'

Shocked silence at his two-letter word. The script girl swallows bravely.

'I'm sorry, sir, our directive is to do the social sequence exactly as scripted. We're having to respool the segments we did last week, Mister Hopkins is very angry with me.'

'Who the hell is Hopkins? Where is he?'

'Oh, please, Paul. Please.'

Paul unwraps himself, saunters back. The holocam crew nervously check their angles. The GTX boardroom has a foible about having things pointed at them and theirs. Cold shivers, when the image of an Isham nearly went onto the world beam beside that Dialadinner.

Worse yet. Paul has no respect for the sacred schedules which are now a full-time job for ferret boy up at headquarters. Paul keeps forgetting to bring her back on time and poor Hopkins can't cope.

So pretty soon the boardroom data-ball has an urgent personal action-tab for Mr. Isham senior. They do it the gentle way, at first.

'I can't today, Paul.'

'Why not?'

'They say I have to, it's very important.'

He strokes the faint gold down on her narrow back. Under Carbondale, Pa., a blind mole-woman shivers.

'Important. Their importance. Making more gold. Can't you see? To them you're just a thing to get scratch with. A huckster. Are you going to let them screw you, Dee? Are you?'

'Oh, Paul –'

He doesn't know it but he's seeing a weirdie; Remotes aren't hooked up to flow tears.

'Just say no, Dee. No. Integrity. You have to.'

'But they say, it's my job –'

'You won't believe I can take care of you, Dee, baby, baby, you're letting them rip us. You have to choose. Tell them, no.'

'Paul … I w-will …'

And she does. Brave little Delphi (insane P. Burke). Saying 'No, please, I promised, Paul.'

They try some more, still gently.

'Paul, Mr. Hopkins told me the reason they don't want us to be together so much. It's because of who you are, your father.'

She thinks her father is like Mr. Cantle, maybe.

'Oh great. Hopkins. I'll fix him. Listen, I can't think about Hopkins now. Ken came back today, he found out something.'

They are lying on the high Andes meadow watching his friends dive their singing kites.

'Would you believe, on the coast the police have electrodes in their heads?'

She stiffens in his arms.

'Yeah, weird. I thought they only used PPs on criminals and the army. Don't you see, Dee – something has to be going on. Some movement. Maybe somebody's organizing. How can we find out?' He pounds the ground behind her. 'We should make contact! If we could only find out.'

'The, the news?' she asks distractedly. 'The news.' He laughs. 'There's nothing in the news except what they want people to know. Half the country could burn up and nobody would know it if they didn't want. Dee, can't you take what I'm explaining to you? They've got the whole world programmed! Total control of communication. They've got everybody's minds wired in to think what they show them and want what, they give them and they give them what they're programmed to want – you can't break in or out of it, you can't get hold of it anywhere. I don't think they even have a plan except to keep things going round and round – and God knows what's happening to the people or the earth or the other planets, maybe. One great big vortex[1] of lies and garbage pouring round and round getting bigger and bigger and nothing can ever change. If people don't wake up soon we're through!'

He pounds her stomach, softly.

'You have to break out, Dee.'

'I'll try, Paul, I will –'

'You're mine. They can't have you.'

1 vortex: swirling mass of sth.

And he goes to see Hopkins, who is indeed cowed.

But that night up under Carbondale the fatherly Mr. Cantle goes to see P. Burke.

P. Burke? On a cot in a utility robe like a dead camel in a tent, she cannot at first comprehend that he is telling her to break it off with Paul. P. Burke has never seen Paul. Delphi sees Paul. The fact is, P. Burke can no longer clearly recall that she exists apart from Delphi.

Mr. Cantle can scarcely believe it either but he tries.

He points out the futility, the potential embarrassment for Paul. That gets a dim stare from the bulk on the bed. Then he goes into her duty to GTX, her job, isn't she grateful for the opportunity, etcetera. He's very persuasive.

The cobwebby mouth of P. Burke opens and croaks.

'No.'

Nothing more seems to be forthcoming.

Mr. Cantle isn't dense, he knows an immovable obstacle when he bumps one. He also knows an irresistible force: GTX. The simple solution is to lock the waldo-cabinet until Paul gets tired of waiting for Delphi to wake up. But the cost, the schedules! And there's something odd here ... he eyes the corporate asset hulking on the bed and his hunch-sense prickles.

You see, Remotes don't love. They don't have real sex, the circuits designed that out from the start. So it's been assumed that it's Paul who is diverting himself or something with the pretty little body in Chile. P. Burke can only be doing what comes natural to any ambitious gutter-meat. It hasn't occurred to anyone that they're dealing with the real hairy thing whose shadow is blasting out of every holoshow on earth.

Love?

Mr. Cantle frowns. The idea is grotesque. But his instinct for the fuzzy line is strong; he will recommend flexibility.

And so, in Chile:

'Darling, I don't have to work tonight! And Friday too – isn't that right, Mr. Hopkins?'

‘Oh, great. When does she come up for parole?’

‘Mr. Isham, please be reasonable. Our schedule – surely your own production people must be needing you?’

This happens to be true. Paul goes away. Hopkins stares after him wondering distastefully why an Isham wants to ball a waldo. (How sound are those boardroom belly-fears – garble creeps, creeps in!) It never occurs to Hopkins that an Isham might not know what Delphi is.

Especially with Davy crying because Paul has kicked him out of Delphi’s bed. Delphi’s bed is under a real window.

‘Stars,’ Paul says sleepily. He rolls over, pulling Delphi on top. ‘Are you aware that this is one of the last places on earth where people can see the stars? Tibet, too, maybe.’

‘Paul …’

‘Go to sleep. I want to see you sleep.’

‘Paul, I … I sleep so hard, I mean, it’s a joke how hard I am to wake up. Do you mind?’

‘Yes.’

But finally, fearfully, she must let go. So that five thousand miles north a crazy spent creature can crawl out to gulp concentrates and fall on her cot. But not for long. It’s pink dawn when Delphi’s eyes open to find Paul’s arms around her, his voice saying rude, tender things. He’s been kept awake. The nerveless little statue that was her Delphi-body nuzzled him in the night.

Insane hope rises, is fed a couple of nights later when he tells her she called his name in her sleep.

And that day Paul’s arms keep her from work and Hopkins’ wails go up to headquarters where the sharp-faced lad is working his sharp tailbone off packing Delphi’s program. Mr. Cantle refuses that one. But next week it happens again, to a major client. And ferret-face has connections on the technical side.

Now you can see that when you have a field of complexly heterodyned energy modulations tuned to a demand-point like Delphi there are many problems of standwaves and lashback and skiffle of all sorts which are normally balanced out with ease by the technology of the future. By the same token they can be delicately[1] unbalanced too, in ways that feed back into the waldo operator with striking results.

'Darling – what the hell! What's wrong? DELPHI!'

Helpless shrieks, writhings. Then the Rima-bird is lying wet and limp in his arms, her eyes enormous.

'I ... I wasn't supposed to ...' she gasps faintly. 'They told me not to ...'

'Oh my god – Delphi.'

And his hard fingers are digging in her thick yellow hair. Electronically knowledgeable fingers. They freeze.

'You're a doll! You're one of those. PP implants. They control you. I should have known. Oh God, I should have known.'

'No, Paul,' she's sobbing. 'No, no, no –'

'Damn them. Damn them, what they've done – you're not your –'

He's shaking her, crouching over her in the bed and jerking her back and forth, glaring at the pitiful beauty.

'No!' She pleads (it's not true, that dark bad dream back there). 'I'm Delphi!'

'My father. Filth, pigs – damn them, damn them, damn them.'

'No, no,' she babbles. 'They were good to me –' P. Burke underground mouthing, 'They were good to me – AAH-AAAAH!'

Another agony skewers her. Up north the sharp young man wants to make sure this so-tiny interference works. Paul can scarcely hang onto her, he's crying too. 'I'll kill them.'

His Dephi, a wired-up slave! Spikes in her brain, electronic shackles in his bird's heart. Remember when those savages burned Rima alive?

'I'll kill the man that's doing this to you.'

He's still saying it afterward but she doesn't hear. She's sure he hates her now, all she wants is to die. When she finally understands

1 delicately: very carefully

that the fierceness[1] is tenderness[2] she thinks it's a miracle. He knows – and he still loves!

How can she guess that he's got it a little bit wrong?

You can't blame Paul. Give him credit that he's even heard about pleasure-pain implants and snoops, which by their nature aren't mentioned much by those who know them most intimately. That's what he thinks is being used on Delphi, something to control her. And to listen – he burns at the unknown ears in their bed.

Of waldo-bodies and objects like P. Burke he has heard nothing.

So it never crosses his mind as he looks down at his violated bird, sick with fury and love, that he isn't holding all of her. Do you need to be told the mad resolve[3] jelling[4] in him now?

To free Delphi.

How? Well, he is after all Paul Isham III. And he even has an idea where the GTX neurolab is. In Carbondale.

But first things have to be done for Delphi, and for his own stomach. So he gives her back to Hopkins and departs in a restrained and discreet way. And the Chile staff is grateful and do not understand that his teeth don't normally show so much.

And a week passes in which Delphi is a very good, docile little ghost. They let her have the load of wildflowers Paul sends and the bland loving notes. (He's playing it coolly.) And up in headquarters weasel boy feels that his destiny has clicked a notch onward and floats the word up that he's handy with little problems.

And no one knows what P. Burke thinks in any way whatever, except that Miss Fleming catches her flushing her food down the can and next night she faints in the pool. They haul her out and stick her with IVs. Miss Fleming frets[5], she's seen expressions like that before. But she wasn't around when crazies who called themselves Followers of the Fish looked through flames to life everlasting. P. Burke is seeing Heaven on the far side of death, too. Heaven is

1 fierceness: displaying anger or aggression **2** tenderness: gentleness and kindness **3** resolve (n): *Entschlossenheit* **4** jell: *Form annehmen* **5** fret: worry

spelled P-a-u-1, but the idea's the same. I will die and be born again in Delphi.

Garbage, electronically speaking. No way.

Another week and Paul's madness has become a plan. (Remember, he does have friends.) He smolders, watching his love paraded by her masters. He turns out a scorching sequence for his own show. And finally, politely, he requests from Hopkins a morsel of his bird's free time, which duly arrives.

'I thought you didn't want me any more,' she's repeating as they wing over mountain flanks in Paul's suncar. 'Now you know –'

'Look at me!'

His hand covers her mouth and he's showing her a lettered card.

DON'T TALK THEY CAN HEAR EVERYTHING WE SAY. I'M TAKING YOU AWAY NOW.

She kisses his hand. He nods urgently, flipping the card.

DON'T BE AFRAID. I CAN STOP THE PAIN IF THEY TRY TO HURT YOU.

With his free hand he shakes out a silvery scrambler-mesh on a power pack. She is dumfounded.

THIS WILL CUT THE SIGNALS AND PROTECT YOU DARLING.

She's staring at him, her head going vaguely from side to side, No.

'Yes!' He grins triumphantly. 'Yes!'

For a moment she wonders. That powered mesh will cut off the field, all right. It will also cut off Delphi. But he is Paul. Paul is kissing her, she can only seek him hungrily as he sweeps the suncar through a pass.

Ahead is an old jet ramp with a shiny bullet waiting to go. (Paul also has credits and a Name.) The little GTX patrol courier is built for nothing but speed. Paul and Delphi wedge in behind the pilot's extra fuel tank and there's no more talking when the torches start to scream.

They're screaming high over Quito before Hopkins starts to worry. He wastes another hour tracking the beeper on Paul's suncar. The suncar is sailing a pattern out to sea. By the time they're sure it's empty and Hopkins gets on the hot flue to headquarters the fugitives are a sourceless howl about Carib West.

Up at headquarters weasel boy gets the squeal. His first impulse is to repeat his previous play but then his brain snaps to. This one is too hot. Because, see, although in the long run they can make P. Burke do anything at all except maybe live, instant emergencies can be tricky. And – Paul Isham III.

'Can't you order her back?'

They're all in the GTX tower monitor station, Mr. Cantle and ferret-face and Joe and a very neat man who is Mr. Isham senior's personal eyes and ears.

'No sir,' Joe says doggedly. 'We can read channels, particularly speech, but we can't interpolate[1] organized patterns. It takes the waldo op to send one-to-one –'

'What are they saying?'

'Nothing at the moment, sir.' The console jockey's eyes are closed. 'I believe they are, ah, embracing.'

'They're not answering,' a traffic monitor says. 'Still heading zero zero three zero – due north, sir.'

'You're certain Kennedy is alerted not to fire on them?' the neat man asks anxiously.

'Yes sir.'

'Can't you just turn her off?' The sharp-faced lad is angry. 'Pull that pig out of the controls!'

'If you cut the transmission cold you'll kill the Remote,' Joe explains for the third time. 'Withdrawal has to be phased right, you have to fade over to the Remote's own autonomies[2]. Heart, breathing, cerebellum[3] would go blooey. If you pull Burke out you'll probably finish her too. It's a fantastic cybersystem, you don't want to do that.'

'The investment.' Mr. Cantle shudders.

1 interpolate sth.: insert sth. into sth. else **2** autonomy: area with self-government **3** cerebellum: part of the brain that controls movement

Weasel boy puts his hand on the console jock's shoulder, it's the contact who arranged the No-no effect for him.

'We can at least give them a warning signal, sir.' He licks his lips, gives the neat man his sweet ferret smile. 'We know that does no damage.'

Joe frowns, Mr. Cantle sighs. The neat man is murmuring into his wrist. He looks up. 'I am authorized,' he says reverently, 'I am authorized to, ah, direct a signal. If this is the only course. But minimal, minimal.'

Sharp-face squeezes his man's shoulder.

In the silver bullet shrieking over Charleston Paul feels Delphi arch in his arms. He reaches for the mesh, hot for action. She thrashes, pushing at his hands, her eyes roll. She's afraid of that mesh despite the agony. (And she's right.) Frantically Paul fights her in the cramped space, gets it over her head. As he turns the power up she burrows free under his arm and the spasm fades.

'They're calling you again, Mister Isham!' the pilot yells.

'Don't answer. Darling, keep this over your head damn it how can I –'

An AX90 barrels over their nose, there's a flash.

'Mister Isham! Those are Air Force jets!'

'Forget it,' Paul shouts back. 'They won't fire. Darling, don't be afraid.'

Another AX90 rocks them.

'Would you mind pointing your pistol at my head where they can see it, sir?' the pilot howls.

Paul does so. The AX90s take up escort formation around them. The pilot goes back to figuring how he can collect from GTX too, and after Goldsboro AB the escort peels away.

'Holding the same course,' Traffic is reporting to the group around the monitor. 'Apparently they've taken on enough fuel to bring them to towerport here.'

'In that case it's just a question of waiting for them to dock.' Mr. Cantle's fatherly manner revives a bit.

'Why can't they cut off that damn freak's life-support,' the sharp young man fumes. 'It's ridiculous.'

'They're working on it,' Cantle assures him.

What they're doing, down under Carbondale, is arguing.

Miss Fleming's watchdog has summoned the bushy man to the waldo room. 'Miss Fleming, you will obey orders.'

'You'll kill her if you try that, sir. I can't believe you meant it, that's why I didn't. We've already fed her enough sedative[1] to affect heart action; if you cut any more oxygen she'll die in there.'

The bushy man grimaces. 'Get Doctor Quine here fast.'

They wait, staring at the cabinet in which a drugged, ugly madwoman fights for consciousness, fights to hold Delphi's eyes open.

High over Richmond the silver pod starts a turn. Delphi is sagged into Paul's arm, her eyes swim up to him.

'Starting down now, baby. It'll be over soon, all you have to do is stay alive, Dee.'

'... Stay alive ...'

The traffic monitor has caught them. 'Sir! They've turned off for Carbondale – Control has contact –'

'Let's go.'

But the headquarters posse is too late to intercept the courier wailing into Carbondale. And Paul's friends have come through again. The fugitives are out through the freight[2] dock[3] and into the neurolab admin port before the guard gets organized. At the elevator Paul's face plus his handgun get them in.

'I want Doctor – what's his name, Dee? Dee!'

'... Tesla ...' She's reeling on her feet.

'Doctor Tesla. Take me down to Tesla, fast.'

1 sedative: sth. taken to make sb. calm or sleepy **2** freight: sth. transported in large amounts by truck, train, ship or aircraft **3** dock: place where a ship rests in a port

Intercoms are squalling around them as they whoosh down, Paul's pistol in the guard's back. When the door slides open the bushy man is there.

'I'm Tesla.'

'I'm Paul Isham. Isham. You're going to take your flaming implants out of this girl – now. Move!'

'What?'

'You heard me. Where's your operating room? Go!'

'But –'

'Move! Do I have to burn somebody?'

Paul waves the weapon at Dr. Quine, who has just appeared.

'No, no,' says Tesla hurriedly. 'But I can't, you know. It's impossible, there'll be nothing left.'

'You screaming well can, right now. You mess up and I'll kill you,' says Paul murderously. 'Where is it, there? And wipe the feke[1] that's on her circuits now.'

He's backing them down the hall, Delphi heavy on his arm. 'Is this the place, baby? Where they did it to you?'

'Yes,' she whispers, bunking at a door. 'Yes ...'

Because it is, see. Behind that door is the very suite where she was born.

Paul herds them through it into a gleaming hall. An inner door opens and a nurse and a gray man rush out. And freeze.

Paul sees there's something special about that inner door. He crowds them past it and pushes it open and looks in.

Inside is a big mean-looking cabinet with its front door panels ajar.

And inside that cabinet is a poisoned carcass to whom something wonderful, unspeakable, is happening. Inside is P. Burke the real living woman who knows that HE is there, coming closer – Paul whom she had fought to reach through forty thousand miles of ice – PAUL is here! – is yanking at the waldo doors –

The doors tear open and a monster rises up.

1 feke: (here) ugly thing

'Paul darling!' croaks the voice of love and the arms of love reach for him.

And he responds.

Wouldn't you, if a gaunt she-golem flab-naked and spouting wires and blood came at you clawing with metal studded paws –

'Get away!' He knocks wires.

It doesn't much matter which wires, P. Burke has so to speak her nervous system hanging out. Imagine somebody jerking a handful of your medulla[1] –

She crashes onto the floor at his feet, flopping and roaring 'PAUL-PAUL-PAUL' in rictus[2].

It's doubtful he recognizes his name or sees her life coming out of her eyes at him. And at the last it doesn't go to him. The eyes find Delphi, fainting by the doorway, and die.

Now of course Delphi is dead, too.

There's total silence as Paul steps away from the thing by his foot.

'You killed her,' Tesla says. 'That was her.'

'Your control.' Paul is furious, the thought of that monster fastened into little Delphi's brain nauseates him. He sees her crumpling and holds out his arms. Not knowing she is dead.

And Delphi comes to him.

One foot before the other, not moving very well – but moving. Her darling face turns up. Paul is distracted by the terrible quiet, and when he looks down he sees only her tender little neck.

'Now you get the implants out,' he warns them. Nobody moves.

'But, she's dead,' Miss Fleming whispers wildly.

Paul feels Delphi's life under his hand, they're talking about their monster. He aims his pistol at the gray man.

'You. If we aren't in your surgery when I count three I'm burning off this man's leg.'

1 medulla (n): inner part of an organ, usu. the lowest part of the brain **2** in rictus: (here) with a frozen unnatural expression

'Mr. Isham,' Tesla says desperately, 'you have just killed the person who animated the body you call Delphi. Delphi herself is dead. If you release your arm you'll see what I say is true.'

The tone gets through. Slowly Paul opens his arm, looks down.

'Delphi?'

She totters, sways, stays upright. Her face comes slowly up.

'Paul ...' Tiny voice.

'Your crotty tricks,' Paul snarls at them. 'Move!'

'Look at her eyes,' Dr. Quine croaks.

They look. One of Delphi's pupils fills the iris, her lips writhe weirdly.

'Shock.' Paul grabs her to him. 'Fix her!' He yells at them, aiming at Tesla.

'For God's sake ... bring it in the lab.' Tesla quavers[1].

'Goodbye-bye,' says Delphi clearly. They lurch down the hall, Paul carrying her, and meet a wave of people.

Headquarters has arrived.

Joe takes one look and dives for the waldo room, running into Paul's gun.

'Oh no, you don't.'

Everybody is yelling. The little thing in his arm stirs, says plaintively, 'I'm Delphi.'

And all through the ensuing jabber and ranting she hangs on, keeps it up, the ghost of P. Burke or whatever whispering crazily, 'Paul ... Paul ... Please, I'm Delphi ... Paul?'

'I'm here, darling, I'm here.' He's holding her in the nursing bed. Tesla talks, talks, talks unheard.

'Paul ... don't sleep ...' the ghost-voice whispers. Paul is in agony, he will not accept, WILL NOT believe.

Tesla runs down.

And then near midnight Delphi says roughly, 'Ag-ag-ag –' and slips onto the floor, making a rough noise like a seal.

1 quaver: shake or tremble while doing sth.

Paul screams. There's more of the ag-ag business and more gruesome convulsive disintegrations, until by two in the morning Delphi is nothing but a warm little bundle of vegetative functions hitched to some expensive hardware – the same that sustained her before her Life began. Joe has finally persuaded Paul to let him at the waldo-cabinet. Paul stays by her long enough to see her face change in a dreadfully alien and coldly convincing way, and then he stumbles out bleakly through the group in Tesla's office.

Behind him Joe is working wet-faced, sweating to reintegrate the fantastic complex of circulation, respiration[1], endocrines, mid-brain homeostases[2], the patterned flux that was a human being – it's like saving an orchestra abandoned in midair. Joe is also crying a little; he alone had truly loved P. Burke. P. Burke, now a dead pile on a table, was the greatest cybersystem he has ever known, and he never forgets her.

The end, really.

You're curious?

Sure, Delphi lives again. Next year she's back on the yacht getting sympathy for her tragic breakdown. But there's a different chick in Chile, because while Delphi's new operator is competent[3], you don't get two P. Burkes in a row – for which GTX is duly grateful.

The real belly-bomb of course is Paul. He was young, see. Fighting abstract wrong. Now life has clawed into him and he goes through gut rage and grief and grows in human wisdom and resolve. So much so that you won't be surprised, some time later, to find him – where?

In the GTX boardroom, dummy. Using the advantage of his birth to radicalize the system. You'd call it 'boring from within.'

That's how he put it, and his friends couldn't agree more. It gives them a warm, confident feeling to know that Paul is up there. Sometimes one of them who's still around runs into him and gets a big hello.

And the sharp-faced lad?

1 respiration: breathing **2** homeostasis: stability **3** competent: having the skill to do sth.

Oh, he matures too. He learns fast, believe it. For instance, he's the first to learn that an obscure GTX research unit is actually getting something with their loopy temporal anomalizer[1] project. True, he doesn't have a physics background, and he's bugged quite a few people. But he doesn't really learn about that until the day he stands where somebody points him during a test run – and wakes up lying on a newspaper headlined NIXON UNVEILS PHASE TWO.

Lucky he's a fast learner.

Believe it, zombie. When I say growth I mean growth. Capital appreciation[2]. You can stop sweating. There's a great future there.

1 anomalizer: sth. that goes from standard or normal **2** appreciation: increase in value

Connor Willumsen

A Journey through a Dystopian Future

Connor Willumsen is a Canadian artist who comes originally from Calgary, Alberta. He began making comics while attending the School of Visual Arts in NYC. He has drawn stories for Marvel Comics and DC Comics among others. His graphic novel *Anti-Gone* (2017) is set in a post-global-warming society, which seems neither destroyed nor stable. Cities are under water, but the economy still works. On the following pages are a few scenes from *Anti-Gone*.

Imagine much of the world had been submerged after global warming. How do you think humans might adapt to the new world? How might stability be achieved in a post-catastrophic world? How much freedom do you think individuals might have?

The annotations below are intended for the text on p. 78:
evidently: obviously
intelligence committee: *Geheimdienstausschuss*
leak: *bekannt werden*
nude: naked person
catch sb.'s eye: to attract sb.'s attention
hi-def (infml) = high definition: *hohe Auflösung*
nah (infml): *Ach was!*
declassify sth.: *etwas freigeben*

DO YOU LIKE READING?
EVIDENTLY.
MAY I...
ASK WHAT YOU ARE READING?
YOU MAY.
FLIP
WHAT..
ARE YOU READING?
HEY ARE THESE ALL HI-DEF?
MOST DEF.
THE SENATE INTELLIGENCE COMMITTEE REPORT ON LEAKED NUDES.
POLITICS EH?
ANYTHING CATCH YOUR EYE?
I THOUGHT UH,
YOU WEREN'T A PIRATE?
NAH NAH, ALL OF THIS DATA HAS BEEN DECLASSIFIED.
STRICTLY ENTERTAINMENT PURPOSES.
HMM...
I'VE SEEN MOST OF THESE ALREADY...
SOME ARE SPECIAL EDITIONS...
WITH COMMENTARY TRACKS.

ARCA
BIGGER

WOOSH
GALLERIA

THUMP
THUMP
THUMP
THUMP
THUMP
THUMP
THUMP
THUMP
THUMP
THUMP
THUMP

AUTO
REDUCE

Ray Bradbury
A Sound of Thunder

The American author Ray Bradbury (1920–2012) was one of the most productive science-fiction, fantasy and horror writers of our time. Apart from his many science-fiction novels and short stories, he also wrote numerous poems, operas, and plays. His most well-known work is the novel *Fahrenheit 451* (1953), depicting a dystopian society in which possessing and reading books is strictly forbidden. His other works include the short-story collections *The Small Assassin* (1946), *The Martian Chronicles* (1950) and *The Illustrated Man* (1951). During his lifetime, Bradbury received numerous awards, including a Pulitzer Citation in 2007. Many of his works have been adapted into other media from comics to films.

Discuss whether time travel will be possible one day. What elements speak for the possibility, what against?

If you could visit another time, which period would you like to visit? Would you like to change anything in that period? If so, how might this affect the present?

The sign on the wall seemed to quaver[1] under a film of sliding warm water. Eckels felt his eyelids blink over his stare, and the sign burned in this momentary darkness:

TIME SAFARI, INC.
SAFARIS TO ANY YEAR IN THE PAST.
YOU NAME THE ANIMAL.
WE TAKE YOU THERE.
YOU SHOOT IT.

1 quaver: shake, tremor

Warm phlegm[1] gathered in Eckels' throat; he swallowed and pushed it down. The muscles around his mouth formed a smile as he put his hand slowly out upon the air, and in that hand waved a check for ten thousand dollars to the man behind the desk.

'Does this safari guarantee I come back alive?'

'We guarantee nothing,' said the official, 'except the dinosaurs.' He turned. 'This is Mr. Travis, your Safari Guide in the Past. He'll tell you what and where to shoot. If he says no shooting, no shooting. If you disobey[2] instructions, there's a stiff[3] penalty of another ten thousand dollars, plus possible government action, on your return.'

Eckels glanced across the vast office at a mass and tangle[4], a snaking and humming[5] of wires and steel boxes, at an aurora[6] that flickered now orange, now silver, now blue. There was a sound like a gigantic bonfire burning all of Time, all the years and all the parchment[7] calendars, all the hours piled high and set aflame.

A touch of the hand and this burning would, on the instant, beautifully reverse itself. Eckels remembered the wording in the advertisements to the letter. Out of chars[8] and ashes, out of dust and coals, like golden salamanders, the old years, the green years, might leap; roses sweeten the air, white hair turn Irish-black, wrinkles vanish; all, everything fly back to seed, flee death, rush down to their beginnings, suns rise in western skies and set in glorious easts, moons eat themselves opposite to the custom, all and everything cupping[9] one in another like Chinese boxes[10], rabbits into hats, all and everything returning to the fresh death, the seed death, the green death, to the time before the beginning. A touch of a hand might do it, the merest touch of a hand.

'Unbelievable.' Eckels breathed, the light of the Machine on his thin face. 'A real Time Machine.' He shook his head. 'Makes you think. If the election had gone badly yesterday, I might be here now

1 phlegm: *Schleim* **2** disobey sth.: *etwas missachten* **3** stiff: *hart* **4** tangle: mess **5** humming: *Brummen* **6** aurora: *Polarlicht* **7** parchment: *Pergament* **8** char: *Holzkohle* **9** cup sth.: *etwas umschließen* **10** Chinese boxes: *ineinander passende Schachteln*

running away from the results. Thank God Keith won. He'll make a fine President of the United States.'

'Yes,' said the man behind the desk. 'We're lucky. If Deutscher had gotten in, we'd have the worst kind of dictatorship. There's an anti-everything man for you, a militarist, anti-Christ, anti-human, anti-intellectual. People called us up, you know, joking but not joking. Said if Deutscher became President they wanted to go live in 1492. Of course it's not our business to conduct Escapes, but to form Safaris. Anyway, Keith's President now. All you got to worry about is –'

'Shooting my dinosaur,' Eckels finished it for him.

'A *Tyrannosaurus Rex*. The Tyrant Lizard[1], the most incredible monster in history. Sign this release. Anything happens to you, we're not responsible. Those dinosaurs are hungry.'

Eckels flushed angrily. 'Trying to scare me!'

'Frankly, yes. We don't want anyone going who'll panic at the first shot. Six Safari leaders were killed last year, and a dozen hunters. We're here to give you the severest[2] thrill a real hunter ever asked for. Traveling you back sixty million years to bag[3] the biggest game in all of Time. Your personal check's still there. Tear it up.'

Mr. Eckels looked at the check. His fingers twitched.

'Good luck,' said the man behind the desk. 'Mr. Travis, he's all yours.'

They moved silently across the room, taking their guns with them, toward the Machine, toward the silver metal and the roaring[4] light.

First a day and then a night and then a day and then a night, then it was day-night-day-night. A week, a month, a year, a decade! A.D.[5] 2055. A.D. 2019. 1999! 1957! Gone! The Machine roared.

They put on their oxygen helmets[6] and tested the intercoms[7].

1 tyrant lizard: the literal meaning of Tyrannosaurus **2** severe: *schwer, stark*
3 bag sth.: *etwas erbeuten* **4** roaring: *gleißend* **5** A.D.: *nach Christus*
6 oxygen helmet: *Sauerstoffhelm* **7** intercom: *Gegensprechanlage*

Eckels swayed[1] on the padded[2] seat, his face pale, his jaw stiff. He felt the trembling in his arms and he looked down and found his hands tight on the new rifle[3]. There were four other men in the Machine. Travis, the Safari Leader, his assistant, Lesperance, and two other hunters, Billings and Kramer. They sat looking at each other, and the years blazed[4] around them.

'Can these guns get a dinosaur cold?' Eckels felt his mouth saying.

'If you hit them right,' said Travis on the helmet radio. 'Some dinosaurs have two brains, one in the head, another far down the spinal column[5]. We stay away from those. That's stretching luck. Put your first two shots into the eyes, if you can, blind them, and go back into the brain.'

The Machine howled. Time was a film run backward. Suns fled and ten million moons fled after them. 'Think,' said Eckels. 'Every hunter that ever lived would envy us today. This makes Africa seem like Illinois.'

The Machine slowed; its scream fell to a murmur[6]. The Machine stopped. The sun stopped in the sky.

The fog that had enveloped the Machine blew away and they were in an old time, a very old time indeed, three hunters and two Safari Heads with their blue metal guns across their knees.

'Christ isn't born yet,' said Travis, 'Moses has not gone to the mountains to talk with God. The Pyramids are still in the earth, waiting to be cut out and put up. *Remember* that. Alexander, Caesar, Napoleon, Hitler – none of them exists.' The man nodded.

'That' – Mr. Travis pointed – 'is the jungle of sixty million two thousand and fifty-five years before President Keith.'

He indicated a metal path that struck off into green wilderness, over streaming swamp[7], among giant ferns[8] and palms.

'And that,' he said, 'is the Path, laid by Time Safari for your use. It floats six inches above the earth. Doesn't touch so much as one

1 sway: *taumeln* **2** padded: *gepolstert* **3** rifle: *Gewehr* **4** blaze: *aufflammen* **5** spinal column: *Wirbelsäule* **6** murmur: whisper **7** swamp: *Sumpf* **8** fern: *Farn*

grass blade, flower, or tree. It's an anti-gravity[1] metal. Its purpose is to keep you from touching this world of the past in any way. Stay on the Path. Don't go off it. I repeat. *Don't go off.* For *any* reason! If you fall off, there's a penalty. And don't shoot any animal we don't okay.'

'Why?' asked Eckels.

They sat in the ancient wilderness. Far birds' cries blew on a wind, and the smell of tar[2] and an old salt sea, moist grasses, and flowers the color of blood.

'We don't want to change the Future. We don't belong here in the Past. The government doesn't *like* us here. We have to pay big graft[3] to keep our franchise. A Time Machine is finicky[4] business. Not knowing it, we might kill an important animal, a small bird, a roach[5], a flower even, thus destroying an important link in a growing species.'

'That's not clear,' said Eckels.

'All right,' Travis continued, 'say we accidentally kill one mouse here. That means all the future families of this one particular mouse are destroyed, right?'

'Right.'

'And all the families of the families of the families of that one mouse! With a stamp of your foot, you annihilate[6] first one, then a dozen, then a thousand, a million, a *billion* possible mice!'

'So they're dead,' said Eckels. 'So what?'

'So what?' Travis snorted quietly. 'Well, what about the foxes that'll need those mice to survive? For want of ten mice, a fox dies. For want of ten foxes a lion starves. For want of a lion, all manner of insects, vultures, infinite billions of life forms are thrown into chaos and destruction. Eventually it all boils down to this: fifty-nine million years later, a caveman, one of a dozen in the *entire world,* goes hunting wild boar or saber-toothed[7] tiger for food. But you, friend, have *stepped* on all the tigers in that region. By stepping on

1 anti-gravity: *gegen die Schwerkraft* **2** tar: *Teer* **3** graft: *Schmiergeld* **4** finicky: difficult **5** roach: *Küchenschabe* **6** annihilate sth.: completely destroy sth. **7** saber-toothed tiger: *Säbelzahntiger*

one single mouse. So the caveman starves. And the caveman, please note, is not just *any* expendable man, no! He is an *entire future nation.* From his loins would have sprung ten sons. From *their* loins one hundred sons, and thus onward to a civilization. Destroy this one man, and you destroy a race, a people, an entire history of life. It is comparable to slaying some of Adam's grandchildren. The stomp of your foot, on one mouse, could start an earthquake, the effects of which could shake our earth and destinies[1] down through Time, to their very foundations. With the death of that one caveman, a billion others yet unborn are throttled[2] in the womb. Perhaps Rome never rises on its seven hills. Perhaps Europe is forever a dark forest, and only Asia waxes[3] healthy and teeming[4]. Step on a mouse and you crush the Pyramids. Step on a mouse and you leave your print, like a Grand Canyon, across Eternity. Queen Elizabeth might never be born, Washington might not cross the Delaware, there might never be a United States at all. So be careful. Stay on the Path. *Never* step off!'

'I see,' said Eckels. 'Then it wouldn't pay for us even to touch the *grass?*'

'Correct. Crushing certain plants could add up infinitesimally[5]. A little error here would multiply in sixty million years, all out of proportion. Of course maybe our theory is wrong. Maybe Time *can't* be changed by us. Or maybe it can be changed only in little subtle ways. A dead mouse here makes an insect imbalance there, a population disproportion later, a bad harvest further on, a depression, mass starvation, and finally, a change in *social* temperament in far-flung[6] countries. Something much more subtle, like that. Perhaps only a soft breath, a whisper, a hair, pollen on the air, such a slight, slight change that unless you looked close you wouldn't see it. Who knows? Who really can say he knows? We don't know. We're guessing. But until we do know for certain whether our

1 destiny: *Schicksal* **2** throttle sb.: *jdn. erdrosseln* **3** wax (v): grow
4 teeming: *wimmelnd* **5** infinitesimal: *(hier) unendlich* **6** far-flung: far away

messing around in Time *can* make a big roar or a little rustle[1] in history, we're being careful. This Machine, this Path, your clothing and bodies, were sterilized, as you know, before the journey. We wear these oxygen helmets so we can't introduce our bacteria into an ancient atmosphere.'

'How do we know which animals to shoot?'

'They're marked with red paint,' said Travis. 'Today, before our journey, we sent Lesperance here back with the Machine. He came to this particular era and followed certain animals.'

'Studying them?'

'Right,' said Lesperance. 'I track them through their entire existence, noting which of them lives longest. Very few. How many times they mate. Not often. Life's short. When I find one that's going to die when a tree falls on him, or one that drowns in a tar pit, I note the exact hour, minute, and second. I shoot a paint bomb. It leaves a red patch on his side. We can't miss it. Then I correlate our arrival in the Past so that we meet the Monster not more than two minutes before he would have died anyway. This way, we kill only animals with no future, that are never going to mate again. You see how *careful* we are?'

'But if you come back this morning in Time,' said Eckels eagerly, you must've bumped into *us,* our Safari! How did it turn out? Was it successful? Did all of us get through – alive?'

Travis and Lesperance gave each other a look.

'That'd be a paradox,' said the latter. 'Time doesn't permit that sort of mess – a man meeting himself. When such occasions threaten, Time steps aside. Like an airplane hitting an air pocket. You felt the Machine jump just before we stopped? That was us passing ourselves on the way back to the Future. We saw nothing. There's no way of telling *if* this expedition was a success, *if we* got our monster, or whether all of us – meaning *you,* Mr. Eckels – got out alive.'

Eckels smiled palely.

1 rustle: noise

'Cut that,' said Travis sharply. 'Everyone on his feet!'

They were ready to leave the Machine.

The jungle was high and the jungle was broad and the jungle was the entire world forever and forever. Sounds like music and sounds like flying tents filled the sky, and those were pterodactyls[1] soaring[2] with cavernous gray wings, gigantic bats of delirium and night fever.

Eckels, balanced on the narrow Path, aimed his rifle playfully.

'Stop that!' said Travis. 'Don't even aim for fun, blast you! If your guns should go off –'

Eckels flushed. 'Where's our *Tyrannosaurus?'*

Lesperance checked his wristwatch. 'Up ahead, We'll bisect[3] his trail in sixty seconds. Look for the red paint! Don't shoot till we give the word. Stay on the Path. *Stay on the Path!'*

They moved forward in the wind of morning.

'Strange,' murmured Eckels. 'Up ahead, sixty million years, Election Day over. Keith made President. Everyone celebrating. And here we are, a million years lost, and they don't exist. The things we worried about for months, a lifetime, not even born or thought of yet.'

'Safety catches off, everyone!' ordered Travis. 'You, first shot, Eckels. Second, Billings, Third, Kramer.'

'I've hunted tiger, wild boar, buffalo, elephant, but now, this is *it,'* said Eckels. 'I'm shaking like a kid.'

'Ah,' said Travis. Everyone stopped.

Travis raised his hand. 'Ahead,' he whispered. 'In the mist. There he is. There's His Royal Majesty now.'

The jungle was wide and full of twitterings[4], rustlings[5], murmurs, and sighs. Suddenly it all ceased, as if someone had shut a door.

Silence.

A sound of thunder.

Out of the mist, one hundred yards away, came *Tyrannosaurus Rex*. 'It,' whispered Eckels. 'It ...'

1 pterodactyl: a type of flying reptile **2** soar: rise in air **3** bisect sth.: cross sth.
4 twittering: *Gezwitscher* **5** rustling: *Rascheln*

'Sh!'

It came on great oiled, resilient[1], striding legs. It towered thirty feet above half of the trees, a great evil god, folding its delicate watchmaker's claws close to its oily reptilian chest. Each lower leg was a piston[2], a thousand pounds of white bone, sunk in thick ropes of muscle, sheathed[3] over in a gleam of pebbled skin like the mail[4] of a terrible warrior. Each thigh[5] was a ton of meat, ivory, and steel mesh[6]. And from the great breathing cage of the upper body those two delicate arms dangled out front, arms with hands which might pick up and examine men like toys, while the snake neck coiled[7]. And the head itself, a ton of sculptured stone, lifted easily upon the sky. Its mouth gaped[8], exposing a fence of teeth like daggers. Its eyes rolled, ostrich[9] eggs, empty of all expression save hunger. It closed its mouth in a death grin. It ran, its pelvic bones[10] crushing aside trees and bushes, its taloned[11] feet clawing damp earth, leaving prints six inches deep wherever it settled its weight.

It ran with a gliding ballet step, far too poised and balanced for its ten tons. It moved into a sunlit area warily, its beautifully reptilian hands feeling the air.

'Why, why,' Eckels twitched his mouth. 'It could reach up and grab the moon.'

'Sh!' Travis jerked angrily. 'He hasn't seen us yet.'

'It can't be killed,' Eckels pronounced this verdict quietly, as if there could be no argument. He had weighed the evidence and this was his considered opinion. The rifle in his hands seemed a cap gun. 'We were fools to come. This is impossible.'

'Shut up!' hissed Travis.

'Nightmare.'

'Turn around,' commanded Travis. 'Walk quietly to the Machine. We'll remit[12] half your fee.'

1 resilient: strong **2** piston: *Kolben* **3** sheathe sth.: cover sth. **4** mail: *Rüstung* **5** thigh: upper part of the leg **6** mesh: net **7** coil: *sich winden* **8** gape: *klaffen* **9** ostrich: *Strauß* **10** pelvic bone: *Beckenknochen* **11** taloned: *krallig* **12** remit sth.: return sth.

'I didn't realize it would be this *big*,' said Eckels. 'I miscalculated, that's all. And now I want out.'

'It *sees* us!'

'There's the red paint on its chest!'

The Tyrant Lizard raised itself. Its armored flesh glittered like a thousand green coins. The coins, crusted with slime, steamed. In the slime, tiny insects wriggled, so that the entire body seemed to twitch and undulate[1], even while the monster itself did not move. It exhaled. The stink of raw flesh blew down the wilderness.

'Get me out of here,' said Eckels. 'It was never like this before. I was always sure I'd come through alive. I had good guides, good safaris, and safety. This time, I figured wrong. I've met my match and admit it. This is too much for me to get hold of.'

'Don't run,' said Lesperance. 'Turn around. Hide in the Machine.'

'Yes.' Eckels seemed to be numb. He looked at his feet as if trying to make them move. He gave a grunt of helplessness.

'Eckels!'

He took a few steps, blinking, shuffling[2].

'Not *that* way!'

The Monster, at the first motion, lunged forward with a terrible scream. It covered one hundred yards in six seconds. The rifles jerked up and blazed fire. A windstorm from the beast's mouth engulfed[3] them in the stench of slime and old blood. The Monster roared, teeth glittering with sun.

The rifles cracked again, their sound was lost in shriek[4] and lizard thunder. The great level of the reptile's tail swung up, lashed sideways. Trees exploded in clouds of leaf and branch. The

Monster twitched its jeweler's hands down to fondle[5] at the men, to twist them in half, to crush them like berries, to cram them into its teeth and its screaming throat. Its boulderstone[6] eyes leveled with the men. They saw themselves mirrored. They fired at the metallic eyelids and the blazing black iris.

1 undulate: *sich wellen* **2** shuffle: *schlurfen* **3** engulf sb./sth.: surround sb./sth.
4 shriek: *Geschrei* **5** fondle sb.: grab sb. **6** boulderstone: granite-like

Like a stone idol, like a mountain avalanche[1], *Tyrannosaurus* fell. Thundering, it clutched trees, pulled them with it. It wrenched and tore[2] the metal Path. The men flung themselves back and away. The body hit, ten tons of cold flesh and stone. The guns fired. The Monster lashed its armored tail, twitched its snake jaws, and lay still. A fount of blood spurted from its throat. Somewhere inside, a sac of fluids burst. Sickening gushes drenched the hunters. They stood, red and glistening.

The thunder faded.

The jungle was silent. After the avalanche, a green peace. After the nightmare, morning.

Billings and Kramer sat on the pathway and threw up. Travis and Lesperance stood with smoking rifles, cursing steadily. In the Time Machine, on his face, Eckels lay shivering. He had found his way back to the Path, climbed into the Machine.

Travis came walking, glanced at Eckels, took cotton gauze from a metal box, and returned to the others, who were sitting on the Path.

'Clean up.'

They wiped the blood from their helmets. They began to curse too. The Monster lay, a hill of solid flesh. Within, you could hear the sighs and murmurs as the furthest chambers of it died, the organs malfunctioning, liquids running a final instant from pocket to sac to spleen[3], everything shutting off, closing up forever. It was like standing by a wrecked locomotive or a steam shovel[4] at quitting time, all valves being released or levered tight. Bones cracked; the tonnage of its own flesh, off balance, dead weight, snapped the delicate forearms, caught underneath. The meat settled, quivering[5].

Another cracking sound. Overhead, a gigantic tree branch broke from its heavy mooring, fell. It crashed upon the dead beast with finality.

1 avalanche: *Lawine* **2** tear sth.: break sth. **3** spleen: *Milz* **4** steam shovel: *Dampfbagger* **5** quiver: *zittern*

'There.' Lesperance checked his watch. 'Right on time. That's the giant tree that was scheduled to fall and kill this animal originally.' He glanced at the two hunters. 'You want the trophy picture?'

'What?'

'We can't take a trophy back to the Future. The body has to stay right here where it would have died originally, so the insects, birds, and bacteria can get at it, as they were intended to. Everything in balance. The body stays. But we can take a picture of you standing near it.'

The two men tried to think, but gave up, shaking their heads.

They let themselves be led along the metal Path. They sank wearily[1] into the Machine cushions. They gazed back at the ruined Monster, the stagnating mound, where already strange reptilian birds and golden insects were busy at the steaming armor. A sound on the floor of the Time Machine stiffened them. Eckels sat there, shivering.

'I'm sorry,' he said at last.

"Get up!" cried Travis.

Eckels got up.

'Go out on that Path alone,' said Travis. He had his rifle pointed, 'You're not coming back in the Machine. We're leaving you here!'

Lesperance seized Travis's arm. 'Wait –'

'Stay out of this!' Travis shook his hand away. 'This fool nearly killed us. But it isn't *that* so much, no. It's his *shoes!* Look at them! He ran off the Path. That *ruins* us! We'll forfeit[2]! Thousands of dollars of insurance! We guarantee no one leaves the Path. He left it. Oh, the fool! I'll have to report to the government. They might revoke our license to travel. Who knows *what* he's done to Time, to History!'

'Take it easy, all he did was kick up some dirt.'

'How do we *know?*' cried Travis. 'We don't know anything! It's all a mystery! Get out of here, Eckels!'

Eckels fumbled his shirt. 'I'll pay anything. A hundred thousand dollars!'

1 weary: very tired **2** forfeit: lose sth. because you broke the rules

Travis glared at Eckels' checkbook and spat. 'Go out there. The Monster's next to the Path. Stick your arms up to your elbows in his mouth. Then you can come back with us.'

'That's unreasonable!'

'The Monster's dead, you idiot. The bullets! The bullets can't be left behind. They don't belong in the Past; they might change anything. Here's my knife. Dig them out!'

The jungle was alive again, full of the old tremorings[1] and bird cries. Eckels turned slowly to regard the primeval garbage dump, that hill of nightmares and terror. After a long time, like a sleepwalker he shuffled out along the Path.

He returned, shuddering, five minutes later, his arms soaked and red to the elbows. He held out his hands. Each held a number of steel bullets. Then he fell. He lay where he fell, not moving.

'You didn't have to make him do that,' said Lesperance.

'Didn't I? It's too early to tell.' Travis nudged[2] the still body. 'He'll live. Next time he won't go hunting game like this. Okay.' He jerked his thumb wearily at Lesperance. 'Switch on. Let's go home.'

1492. 1776. 1812.

They cleaned their hands and faces. They changed their caking shirts and pants. Eckels was up and around again, not speaking. Travis glared at him for a full ten minutes.

'Don't look at me,' cried Eckels. 'I haven't done anything.'

'Who can tell?'

'Just ran off the Path, that's all, a little mud on my shoes – what do you want me to do – get down and pray?'

'We might need it. I'm warning you, Eckels, I might kill you yet. I've got my gun ready.'

'I'm innocent. I've done nothing!'

1999. 2000. 2055.

The Machine stopped.

'Get out,' said Travis.

1 tremoring: shaking **2** nudge sb.: *jdn. anstupsen*

The room was there as they had left it. But not the same as they had left it. The same man sat behind the same desk. But the same man did not quite sit behind the same desk. Travis looked around swiftly. 'Everything okay here?' he snapped.

'Fine. Welcome home!'

Travis did not relax. He seemed to be looking through the one high window.

'Okay, Eckels, get out. Don't ever come back.'

Eckels could not move.

'You heard me,' said Travis. 'What're you *staring* at?'

Eckels stood smelling of the air, and there was a thing to the air, a chemical taint[1] so subtle, so slight, that only a faint cry of his subliminal[2] senses warned him it was there. The colors, white, grey, blue, orange, in the wall, in the furniture, in the sky beyond the window, were … were … . And there was a *feel*. His flesh twitched. His hands twitched. He stood drinking the oddness with the pores of his body. Somewhere, someone must have been screaming one of those whistles that only a dog can hear. His body screamed silence in return. Beyond this room, beyond this wall, beyond this man who was not quite the same man seated at this desk that was not quite the same desk … lay an entire world of streets and people. What sort of world it was now, there was no telling. He could feel them moving there, beyond the walls, almost, like so many chess pieces blown in a dry wind …

But the immediate thing was the sign painted on the office wall, the same sign he had read earlier today on first entering. Somehow, the sign had changed:

TYME SEFARI INC.
SEFARIS TU ANY YEER EN THE PAST.
YU NAIM THE ANIMALL.
WEE TAEK YU THAIR.
YU SHOOT ITT.

1 taint: *Beigeschmack* **2** subliminal: *unterbewusst*

Eckels felt himself fall into a chair. He fumbled crazily at the thick slime on his boots. He held up a clod of dirt, trembling, 'No, it can't be. Not a *little* thing like that. No!'

Embedded in the mud, glistening green and gold and black, was a butterfly, very beautiful and very dead.

'Not a little thing like *that!* Not a butterfly!' cried Eckels.

It fell to the floor, an exquisite thing, a small thing that could upset balances and knock down a line of small dominoes and then big dominoes and then gigantic dominoes, all down the years across Time. Eckels' mind whirled. It *couldn't* change things. Killing one butterfly couldn't be *that* important! Could it?

His face was cold. His mouth trembled, asking: 'Who – who won the presidential election yesterday?'

The man behind the desk laughed. 'You joking? You know very well. Deutscher, of course! Who else? Not that fool weakling Keith. We got an iron man now, a man with guts!' The official stopped. 'What's wrong?'

Eckels moaned. He dropped to his knees. He scrabbled at the golden butterfly with shaking fingers. 'Can't we,' he pleaded to the world, to himself, to the officials, to the Machine, 'can't we take it *back*, can't we *make* it alive again? Can't we start over? Can't we –'

He did not move. Eyes shut, he waited, shivering. He heard Travis breathe loud in the room; he heard Travis shift his rifle, click the safety catch, and raise the weapon.

There was a sound of thunder.

Ursula Le Guin
Solitude

Ursula K. Le Guin (1929–2018) was one of the most famous American science-fiction and fantasy writers of our time. She won numerous prizes during her career and was one of the first women to be made a Grand Master of Science Fiction, an honour awarded by the Science Fiction and Fantasy Writers of America. Some of her most famous writings include the 'Earthsea' series (1968–2001), *The Left Hand of Darkness* (1969) and *The Dispossessed* (1974). While Le Guin's writings cover a broad spectrum of topics, many of her works deal with feminist and gender issues as well as the cultural and social structures of society. Another recurrent theme in her work is environmentalism. Le Guin was the first writer to be awarded both the prestigious Hugo and Nebula awards twice for the same novels. The following short story was first published in 1994 .

Imagine a family moves from one culture to another. Discuss how the parents might view the new culture as compared to their children. Then imagine how returning to their original country might be viewed by the two generations.

An addition to 'POVERTY: The Second Report on Eleven-Soro' by Mobile Entselenne'temharyonoterregwis Leaf, by her daughter, Serenity.

My mother, a field ethnologist[1], took the difficulty of learning anything about the people of Eleven-Soro as a personal challenge. The fact that she used her children to meet that challenge might be seen as selfishness or as selflessness. Now that I have read her report I know that she finally thought she had done wrong. Knowing what

1 ethnologist: *Völkerkundler/in*

it cost her, I wish she knew my gratitude to her for allowing me to grow up as a person.

Shortly after a robot probe[1] reported people of the Hainish Descent on the eleventh planet of the Soro system, she joined the orbital crew as back-up for the three First Observers down on-planet. She had spent four years in the tree-cities of nearby Huthu. My brother In Joy Born was eight years old and I was five; she wanted a year or two of ship duty so we could spend some time in a Hainish-style school. My brother had enjoyed the rainforests of Huthu very much, but though he could brachiate[2] he could barely read, and we were all bright blue with skin-fungus[3]. While Borny learned to read and I learned to wear clothes and we all had anti-fungus treatments, my mother became as intrigued by Eleven-Soro as the Observers were frustrated by it.

All this is in her report, but I will say it as I learned it from her, which helps me remember and understand. The language had been recorded by the probe and the Observers had spent a year learning it. The many dialectical variations excused their accents and errors, and they reported that language was not a problem. Yet there was a communication problem. The two men found themselves isolated, faced with suspicion[4] or hostility, unable to form any connection with the native men, all of whom lived in solitary houses as hermits[5] or in pairs. Finding communities of adolescent males, they tried to make contact with them, but when they entered the territory of such a group the boys either fled or rushed desperately at them trying to kill them. The women, who lived in what they called 'dispersed[6] villages', drove them away with volleys of stones as soon as they came anywhere near the houses. 'I believe,' one of them reported, 'that the only community activity of the Sorovians is throwing rocks at men.'

1 probe: *Sonde* **2** brachiate: *hangeln* **3** skin-fungus: *Hautpilz* **4** suspicion: the feeling that you cannot trust sb./sth. **5** hermit: *Einsiedler* **6** dispersed: *verteilt*

Neither of them succeeded in having a conversation of more than three exchanges with a man. One of them mated with a woman who came by his camp; he reported that though she made unmistakable and insistent advances, she seemed disturbed by his attempts to converse, refused to answer his questions, and left him, he said, 'as soon as she got what she came for'.

The woman Observer was allowed to settle in an unused house in a 'village' (auntring) of seven houses. She made excellent observations of daily life, insofar as she could see any of it, and had several conversations with adult women and many with children; but she found that she was never asked into another woman's house, nor expected to help or ask for help in any work. Conversation concerning normal activities was unwelcome to the other women; the children, her only informants, called her Aunt Crazy-Jabber. Her aberrant[1] behavior caused increasing distrust and dislike among the women, and they began to keep their children away from her. She left. 'There's no way,' she told my mother, 'for an adult to learn anything. They don't ask questions, they don't answer questions. Whatever they learn, they learn when they're children.'

Aha! said my mother to herself, looking at Borny and me. And she requested a family transfer to Eleven-Soro with Observer status. The Stabiles interviewed her extensively by ansible[2], and talked with Borny and even with me – I don't remember it, but she told me I told the Stabiles all about my new stockings – and agreed to her request. The ship was to stay in close orbit, with the previous Observers in the crew, and she was to keep radio contact with it, daily if possible.

I have a dim[3] memory of the tree-city, and of playing with what must have been a kitten or a ghole-kit on the ship; but my first clear memories are of our house in the auntring. It is half underground, half aboveground, with wattle-and-daub walls[4]. Mother and I are standing outside it in the warm sunshine. Between us is a big

1 aberrant: *abnormal* **2** ansible: fictional device for communication **3** dim: not strong **4** wattle-and-daub wall: *Flechtwerkwand*

mudpuddle[1], into which Borny pours water from a basket; then he runs off to the creek[2] to get more water. I muddle the mud with my hands, deliciously, till it is thick and smooth. I pick up a big double handful and slap it onto the walls where the sticks show through. Mother says, 'That's good! That's right!' in our new language, and I realize that this is work, and I am doing it. I am repairing the house. I am making it right, doing it right. I am a competent person.

I have never doubted that, so long as I lived there.

We are inside the house at night, and Borny is talking to the ship on the radio, because he misses talking the old language, and anyway he is supposed to tell them stuff. Mother is making a basket and sweating at the split reeds[3]. I am singing a song to drown out Borny so nobody in the auntring hears him talking funny, and anyway I like singing. I learned this song this afternoon in Hyuru's house. I play every day with Hyuru. 'Be aware, listen, listen, be aware,' I sing. When Mother stops swearing she listens, and then she turns on the recorder. There is a little fire still left from cooking dinner, which was lovely pigi root, I never get tired of pigi. It is dark and warm and smells of pigi and of burning duhur, which is a strong, sacred smell to drive out magic and bad feelings, and as I sing 'Listen, be aware', I get sleepier and sleepier and lean against Mother, who is dark and warm and smells like Mother, strong and sacred, full of good feelings.

Our daily life in the auntring was repetitive. On the ship, later, I learned that people who live in artificially complicated situations call such a life 'simple'. I never knew anybody, anywhere I have been, who found life simple. I think a life or a time looks simple when you leave out the details, the way a planet looks smooth, from orbit.

Certainly our life in the auntring was easy, in the sense that our needs came easily to hand. There was plenty of food to be gathered or grown and prepared and cooked, plenty of temas to pick and rett and spin and weave for clothes and bedding plenty of reeds to make baskets and thatch with; we children had other children to play

1 mud puddle: *Schlammpfütze* **2** creek: river **3** reed: *Schilf*

with, mothers to look after us, and a great deal to learn. None of this is simple, though it's all easy enough, when you know how to do it, when you are aware of the details.

It was not easy for my mother. It was hard for her, and complicated. She had to pretend she knew the details while she was learning them, and had to think how to report and explain this way of living to people in another place who didn't understand it. For Borny it was easy until it got hard because he was a boy. For me it was all easy. I learned the work and played with the children and listened to the mothers sing.

The First Observer had been quite right: there was no way for a grown woman to learn how to make her soul. Mother couldn't go listen to another mother sing, it would have been too strange. The aunts all knew she hadn't been brought up well, and some of them taught her a good deal without her realizing it. They had decided her mother must have been irresponsible[1] and had gone on scouting[2] instead of settling in an auntring so that her daughter didn't get educated properly. That's why even the most aloof[3] of the aunts always let me listen with their children, so that I could become an educated person. But of course they couldn't ask another adult into their houses. Borny and I had to tell her all the songs and stories we learned, and then she would tell them to the radio, or we told them to the radio while she listened to us. But she never got it right, not really. How could she, trying to learn it after she'd grown up, and after she'd always lived with magicians?

'Be aware!' she would imitate my solemn[4] and probably irritating imitation of the aunts and the big girls. 'Be aware! How many times a day do they say that? Be aware of what? They aren't aware of what the ruins are, their own history – they aren't aware of each other! They don't even talk to each other! Be aware, indeed!'

When I told her the stories of the Before Time that Aunt Sadne and Aunt Noyit told their daughters and me, she often heard the

1 irresponsible: *unverantwortlich* **2** scout: *eine Erkundungstour machen*
3 aloof: keeping people at a distance **4** solemn: *feierlich*

wrong things in them. I told her about the People, and she said, 'Those are the ancestors[1] of the people here now.' When I said, 'There aren't any people here now,' she didn't understand. 'There are persons here now,' I said, but she still didn't understand.

Borny liked the story about the Man Who Lived with Women, how he kept some women in a pen, the way some persons keep rats in a pen for eating, and all of them got pregnant, and they each had a hundred babies, and the babies grew up as horrible monsters and ate the man and the mothers and each other. Mother explained to us that that was a parable of the human overpopulation of this planet thousands of years ago. 'No, it's not,' I said, 'it's a moral story.' – 'Well, yes,' Mother said. 'The moral is, don't have too many babies.' – 'No, it's not,' I said. 'Who could have a hundred babies even if they wanted to? The man was a sorceror[2]. He did magic. The women did it with him. So of course their children were monsters.'

The key, of course, is the word 'tekell', which translates so nicely into the Hainish word 'magic', an art or power that violates natural law. It was hard for Mother to understand that some persons truly consider most human relationships unnatural; that marriage, for instance, or government, can be seen as an evil spell woven by sorcerors. It is hard for her people to believe magic.

The ship kept asking if we were all right, and every now and then a Stabile would hook up[3] the ansible to our radio and grill Mother and us. She always convinced them that she wanted to stay, for despite her frustrations, she was doing the work the First Observers had not been able to do, and Borny and I were happy as mudfish[4], all those first years. I think Mother was happy too, once she got used to the slow pace[5] and the indirect way she had to learn things. She was lonely, missing other grown-ups to talk to, and told us that she would have gone crazy without us. If she missed sex she never showed it. I think, though, that her Report is not very complete about sexual matters, perhaps because she was troubled by them.

1 ancestors: *Vorfahren* **2** sorceror (usu: sorcerer): *Zauberer/in* **3** hook sth. up: *etwas verbinden* **4** mudfish: *Schlammfisch* **5** pace: *Tempo*

I know that when we first lived in the auntring, two of the aunts, Hedimi and Behyu, used to meet to make love, and Behyu courted my mother; but Mother didn't understand, because Behyu wouldn't talk the way Mother wanted to talk. She couldn't understand having sex with a person whose house you wouldn't enter.

Once when I was nine or so, and had been listening to some of the older girls, I asked her why didn't she go out scouting. 'Aunt Sadne would look after us,' I said, hopefully. I was tired of being the uneducated woman's daughter. I wanted to live in Aunt Sadne's house and be just like the other children.

'Mothers don't scout,' she said, scornfully[1], like an aunt.

'Yes, they do, sometimes,' I insisted. 'They have to, or how could they have more than one baby?'

'They go to settled men near the auntring. Behyu went back to the Red Knob Hill Man when she wanted a second child. Sadne goes and sees Downriver Lame Man when she wants to have sex. They know the men around here. None of the mothers scout.'

I realized that in this case she was right and I was wrong, but I stuck to my point. 'Well, why don't you go see Downriver Lame Man? Don't you ever want sex? Migi says she wants it all the time.'

'Migi is seventeen,' Mother said drily. 'Mind your own nose.' She sounded exactly like all the other mothers.

Men, during my childhood, were a kind of uninteresting mystery to me. They turned up a lot in the Before Time stories, and the singing-circle girls talked about them; but I seldom saw any of them. Sometimes I'd glimpse[2] one when I was foraging[3], but they never came near the auntring. In summer the Downriver Lame Man would get lonesome waiting for Aunt Sadne and would come lurking around, not very far from the auntring – not in the bush or down by the river, of course, where he might be mistaken for a rogue[4] and stoned – but out in the open, on the hillsides, where we could all see who he was. Hyuru and Didsu, Aunt Sadne's daughters,

1 scornful: *verächtlich* **2** glimpse sb./sth.: *einen kurzen Blick auf jdn./etwas erhaschen* **3** forage: *Nahrung suchen* **4** rogue: *Schurke*

said she had had sex with him when she went out scouting the first time, and always had sex with him and never tried any of the other men of the settlement.

She had told them, too, that the first child she bore was a boy, and she drowned it, because she didn't want to bring up a boy and send him away. They felt queer[1] about that and so did I, but it wasn't an uncommon thing. One of the stories we learned was about a drowned[2] boy who grew up underwater, and seized his mother when she came to bathe, and tried to hold her under till she too drowned; but she escaped.

At any rate, after the Downriver Lame Man had sat around for several days on the hillsides, singing long songs and braiding and unbraiding his hair, which was long too, and shone black in the sun, Aunt Sadne always went off for a night or two with him, and came back looking cross and self-conscious.

Aunt Noyit explained to me that Downriver Lame Man's songs were magic; not the usual bad magic, but what she called the great good spells. Aunt Sadne never could resist his spells. 'But he hasn't half the charm of some men I've known,' said Aunt Noyit, smiling reminiscently.

Our diet, though excellent, was very low in fat, which Mother thought might explain the rather late onset of puberty; girls seldom menstreated[3] before they were fifteen, and boys often weren't mature till they were considerably older than that. But the women began looking askance[4] at boys as soon as they showed any signs at all of adolescence. First Aunt Hedimi, who was always grim, then Aunt Noyit, then even Aunt Sadne began to turn away from Borny, to leave him out, not answering when he spoke. 'What are you doing playing with the children?' old Aunt Dnemi asked him so fiercely that he came home in tears. He was not quite fourteen.

Sadne's younger daughter Hyuru was my soulmate, my best friend, you would say. Her elder sister Didsu, who was in the singing

1 feel queer: *sich schlecht fühlen* **2** drown: *ertrinken* **3** menstreat = menstruate: *menstruieren* **4** askance: *missbilligend*

circle now, came and talked to me one day, looking serious. 'Borny is very handsome,' she said. I agreed proudly.

'Very big, very strong,' she said, 'stronger than I am.'

I agreed proudly again, and then I began to back away from her.

'I'm not doing magic, Ren,' she said.

'Yes you are,' I said. 'I'll tell your mother!'

Didsu shook her head. 'I'm trying to speak truly. If my fear causes your fear, I can't help it. It has to be so. We talked about it in the singing circle. I don't like it,' she said, and I knew she meant it; she had a soft face, soft eyes, she had always been the gentlest of us children. 'I wish he could be a child,' she said. 'I wish I could. But we can't.'

'Go be a stupid old woman, then,' I said, and ran away from her. I went to my secret place down by the river and cried. I took the holies[1] out of my soulbag[2] and arranged them. One holy – it doesn't matter if I tell you – was a crystal that Borny had given me, clear at the top, cloudy purple at the base. I held it a long time and then I gave it back. I dug a hole under a boulder[3], and wrapped the holy in duhur leaves inside a square of cloth I tore out[4] of my kilt, beautiful, fine cloth Hyuru had woven and sewn for me. I tore the square right from the front, where it would show. I gave the crystal back, and then sat a long time there near it. When I went home I said nothing of what Didsu had said. But Borny was very silent, and my mother had a worried look. 'What have you done to your kilt, Ren?' she asked. I raised my head a little and did not answer; she started to speak again, and then did not. She had finally learned not to talk to a person who chose to be silent.

Borny didn't have a soulmate, but he had been playing more and more often with the two boys nearest his age, Ednede who was a year or two older, a slight, quiet boy, and Bit who was only eleven, but boisterous and reckless.

1 holy: *heiliges Ding, Schatz* **2** soulbag: (here) bag with things that are considered spiritual **3** boulder: *Felsbrocken* **4** tear sth. out: *etwas herausreißen*

The three of them went off somewhere all the time. I hadn't paid much attention, partly because I was glad to be rid of Bit. Hyuru and I had been practicing being aware, and it was tiresome to always have to be aware of Bit yelling and jumping around. He never could leave anyone quiet, as if their quietness took something from him. His mother, Hedimi, had educated him, but she wasn't a good singer or story-teller like Sadne and Noyit, and Bit was too restless to listen even to them. Whenever he saw me and Hyuru trying to slow-walk or sitting being aware, he hung around making noise till we got mad and told him to go, and then he jeered[1], 'Dumb girls!'

I asked Borny what he and Bit and Ednede did, and he said, 'Boy stuff.'

'Like what?'

'Practicing.'

'Being aware?'

After a while he said, 'No.

'Practicing what, then?'

'Wrestling. Getting strong. For the boygroup.' He looked gloomy, but after a while he said, 'Look,' and showed me a knife he had hidden under his mattress. 'Ednede says you have to have a knife, then nobody will challenge you. Isn't it a beauty?' It was metal, old metal from the People, shaped like a reed, pounded out[2] and sharpened down[3] both edges, with a sharp point. A piece of polished flintshrub[4] wood had been bored[5] and fitted on the handle to protect the hand. 'I found it in an empty man's-house,' he said. 'I made the wooden part.' He brooded[6] over it lovingly. Yet he did not keep it in his soulbag.

'What do you do with it?" I asked, wondering why both edges were sharp, so you'd cut your hand if you used it.

'Keep off attackers,' he said.

'Where was the empty man's-house?'

1 jeer: *spotten* **2** pound out sth.: *etwas heraushämmern* **3** sharpen down sth.: *etwas schärfen* **4** flintshrub: (here) type of wood **5** bore sth.: *etwas bohren* **6** brood: *brüten*

'Way over across Rocky Top.'

'Can I go with you if you go back?'

'No," he said, not unkindly, but absolutely.

'What happened to the man? Did he die?'

'There was a skull in the creek. We think he slipped and drowned.'

He didn't sound quite like Borny. There was something in his voice like a grown-up; melancholy; reserved. I had gone to him for reassurance, but came away more deeply anxious. I went to Mother and asked her, 'What do they do in the boygroups?'

'Perform natural selection,' she said, not in my language but in hers, in a strained tone. I didn't always understand Hainish any more and had no idea what she meant, but the tone of her voice upset me; and to my horror I saw she had begun to cry silently. 'We have to move, Serenity,' she said – she was still talking Hainish without realizing it. 'There isn't any reason why a family can't move, is there? Women just move in and move out as they please. Nobody cares what anybody does. Nothing is anybody's business. Except hounding the boys out of town!'

I understood most of what she said, but got her to say it in my language; and then I said, 'But anywhere we went, Borny would be the same age, and size, and everything.'

'Then we'll leave,' she said fiercely. 'Go back to the ship.'

I drew away from her. I had never been afraid of her before: she had never used magic on me. A mother has great power, but there is nothing unnatural in it, unless it is used against the child's soul.

Borny had no fear of her. He had his own magic. When she told him she intended leaving, he persuaded her out of it. He wanted to go join the boygroup, he said; he'd been wanting to for a year now. He didn't belong in the auntring any more, all women and girls and little kids. He wanted to go live with other boys. Bit's older brother Yit was a member of the boygroup in the Four Rivers Territory, and would look after a boy from his auntring. And Ednede was getting ready to go. And Borny and Ednede and Bit had been talking to some men, recently. Men weren't all ignorant and crazy, the way Mother thought. They didn't talk much, but they knew a lot.

‘What do they know?’ Mother asked grimly

‘They know how to be men,’ Borny said. ‘It’s what I’m going to be.’

‘Not that kind of man – not if I can help it! In Joy Born, you must remember the men on the ship, real men – nothing like these poor, filthy hermits. I can’t let you grow up thinking that that’s what you have to be!’

‘They’re not like that,’ Borny said. ‘You ought to go talk to some of them, Mother.’

‘Don’t be naive,’ she said with an edgy laugh. ‘You know perfectly well that women don’t go to men to talk.’

I knew she was wrong; all the women in the auntring knew all the settled men for three days’ walk around. They did talk with them, when they were out foraging. They only kept away from the ones they didn’t trust; and usually those men disappeared before long. Noyit had told me, ‘Their magic turns on them.’ She meant the other men drove them away or killed them. But I didn’t say any of this, and Borny said only, ‘Well, Cave Cliff Man is really nice. And he took us to the place where I found those People things’ – some ancient artifacts that Mother had been excited about. ‘The men know things the women don’t,’ Borny went on. ‘At least I could go to the boygroup for a while, maybe. I ought to. I could learn a lot! We don’t have any solid information on them at all. All we know anything about is this auntring. I’ll go and stay long enough to get material for our report. I can’t ever come back to either the auntring or the boygroup once I leave them. I’ll have to go to the ship, or else try to be a man. So let me have a real go at it, please, Mother?’

‘I don’t know why you think you have to learn how to be a man,’ she said after a while. ‘You know how already.’

He really smiled then, and she put her arm around him.

What about me? I thought. I don’t even know what the ship is. I want to be here, where my soul is. I want to go on learning to be in the world.

But I was afraid of Mother and Borny, who were both working magic, and so I said nothing and was still, as I had been taught.

Ednede and Borny went off together. Noyit, Ednede's mother, was as glad as Mother was about their keeping company, though she said nothing. The evening before they left, the two boys went to every house in the auntring. It took a long time. The houses were each just within sight or hearing of one or two of the others, with bush and gardens and irrigation ditches and paths in between. In each house the mother and the children were waiting to say goodbye, only they didn't say it; my language has no word for hello or goodbye. They asked the boys in and gave them something to eat, something they could take with them on the way to the Territory. When the boys went to the door everybody in the household came and touched their hand or cheek. I remembered when Yit had gone around the auntring that way. I had cried then, because even though I didn't much like Yit, it seemed so strange for somebody to leave forever, like they were dying. This time I didn't cry; but I kept waking and waking again, until I heard Borny get up before the first light and pick up his things and leave quietly. I know Mother was awake too, but we did as we should do, and lay still while he left, and for a long time after.

I have read her description of what she calls 'An adolescent male leaves the Auntring: a vestigial[1] survival[2] of ceremony.'

She had wanted him to put a radio in his soulbag and get in touch with her at least occasionally. He had been unwilling. 'I want to do it right, Mother. There's no use doing it if I don't do it right.'

'I simply can't handle not hearing from you at all, Borny,' she had said in Hainish.

'But if the radio got broken or taken or something you'd worry a lot more, maybe with no reason at all.'

She finally agreed to wait half a year, till the first rains then she would go to a landmark, a huge rain near the river that marked the southern end of the Territory, and he would try and come to her there. 'But only wait ten days,' he said. 'If I can't come, I can't.' She

1 vestigial: remaining as the last small part of something that used to exist
2 survival: *Überrest*

agreed. She was like a mother with a little baby, I thought, saying yes to everything. That seemed wrong to me; but I thought Borny was right. Nobody ever came back to their mother from boygroup.

But Borny did.

Summer was long, clear, beautiful. I was learning to starwatch; that is when you lie down outside on the open hills in the dry season at night, and find a certain star in the eastern sky, and watch it cross the sky till it sets. You can look away, of course, to rest your eyes, and doze[1], but you try to keep looking back at the star and the stars around it, until you feel the earth turning, until you become aware of how the stars and the world and the soul move together. After the certain star sets, you sleep until dawn wakes you. Then as always you greet the sunrise with aware silence. I was very happy on the hills those warm great nights, those clear dawns. The first time or two Hyuru and I starwatched together, but after that we went alone, and it was better alone.

I was coming back from such a night, along the narrow valley between Rocky Top and Over Home Hill in the first sunlight, when a man came crashing through the bush down onto the path and stood in front of me. 'Don't be afraid,' he said, 'Listen!' He was heavyset, half naked; he stank.

I stood still as a stick. He had said 'Listen!' just as the aunts did, and I listened. 'Your brother and his friend are all right. Your mother shouldn't go there. Some of the boys are in a gang. They'd rape her. I and some others are killing the leaders. It takes a while. Your brother is with the other gang. He's all right. Tell her. Tell me what I said.'

I repeated it word for word, as I had learned to do when I listened.

'Right. Good,' he said, and took off up the steep slope on his short, powerful legs, and was gone.

Mother would have gone to the Territory right then, but I told the man's message to Noyit, too, and she came to the porch of our house to speak to Mother. I listened to her, because she was telling things I didn't know well and Mother didn't know at all. Noyit was

1 doze: *dösen*

a small, mild woman, very like her son Ednede; she liked teaching and singing, so the children were always around her place. She saw Mother was getting ready for a journey. She said, 'House on the Skyline Man says the boys are all right.' When she saw Mother wasn't listening, she went on, she pretended to be talking to me, because women don't teach women: 'He says some of the men are breaking up the gang. They do that, when the boygroups get wicked[1]. Sometimes there are magicians among them, leaders, older boys, even men who want to make a gang. The settled men will kill the magicians and make sure none of the boys gets hurt. When gangs come out of the Territories, nobody is safe. The settled men don't like that. They see to it that the auntring is safe. So your brother will be all right.'

My mother went on packing pigi-roots into her net.

'A rape is a very, very bad thing for the settled men,' said Noyit to me. 'It means the women won't come to them. If the boys raped some woman, probably the men would kill all the boys.'

My mother was finally listening.

She did not go to the rendezvous with Borny, but all through the rainy season she was utterly miserable. She got sick, and old Dnemi sent Didsu over to dose her with gagberry syrup. She made notes while she was sick, lying on her mattress, about illnesses and medicines and how the older girls had to look after sick women, since grown women did not enter one another's houses. She never stopped working and never stopped worrying about Borny.

Late in the rainy season, when the warm wind had come and the yellow honey-flowers were in bloom on all the hills, the Golden World time, Noyit came by while Mother was working in the garden. 'House on the Skyline Man says things are all right in the boygroup,' she said, and went on.

Mother began to realize then that although no adult ever entered another's house, and adults seldom spoke to one another, and men and women had only brief, often casual relationships, and men lived

1 wicked: *böse*

all their lives in real solitude, still there was a kind of community, a wide, thin, fine network of delicate[1] and certain intention and restraint[2]: a social order. Her reports to the ship were filled with this new understanding. But she still found Sorovian life impoverished[3], seeing these persons as mere survivors, poor fragments of the wreck of something great.

'My dear,' she said – in Hainish; there is no way to say 'my dear' in my language. She was speaking Hainish with me in the house so that I wouldn't forget it entirely. – 'My dear, the explanation of an uncomprehended technology as magic is primitivism. It's not a criticism, merely a description.'

'But technology isn't magic,' I said.

'Yes, it is, in their minds; look at the story you just recorded. Before Time sorcerors who could fly in the air and undersea and underground in magic boxes!"

'In metal boxes,' I corrected.

'In other words, airplanes, tunnels, submarines; a lost technology explained as supernatural.'

'The boxes weren't magic,' I said. 'The people were. They were sorcerors. They used their power to get power over other persons. To live rightly a person has to keep away from magic.'

'That's a cultural imperative, because a few thousand years ago uncontrolled technological expansion led to disaster. Exactly. There's a perfectly rational reason for the irrational taboo.'

I did not know what 'rational' and 'irrational' meant in my language; I could not find words for them. 'Taboo' was the same as 'poisonous.' I listened to my mother because a daughter must learn from her mother, and my mother knew many, many things no other person knew; but my education was very difficult, sometimes. If only there were more stories and songs in her teaching, and not so many words, words that slipped away from me like water through a net!

1 delicate: *zart* **2** restraint: *Zurückhaltung, Beschränkung* **3** impoverished: *verarmt, dürftig*

The Golden Time passed, and the beautiful summer; the Silver Time returned, when the mists lie in the valleys between the hills, before the rains begin; and the rains began, and fell long and slow and warm, day after day after day. We had heard nothing of Borny and Ednede for over a year. Then in the night the soft thrum[1] of rain on the reed roof turned into a scratching at the door and a whisper, 'Shh – it's all right – it's all right.'

We wakened[2] the fire and crouched[3] at it in the dark to talk. Borny had got tall and very thin, like a skeleton with the skin dried on it. A cut across his upper lip had drawn it up into a kind of snarl[4] that bared[5] his teeth, and he could not say p, b, or m. His voice was a man's voice. He huddled at the fire trying to get warmth into his bones. His clothes were wet rags[6]. The knife hung on a cord around his neck. 'It was all right,' he kept saying. 'I don't want to go on there, though.'

He would not tell us much about the year and a half in the boygroup, insisting that he would record a full description when he got to the ship. He did tell us what he would have to do if he stayed on Soro. He would have to go back to the Territory and hold his own among the older boys, by fear and sorcery, always proving his strength, until he was old enough to walk away – that is, to leave the Territory and wander alone till he found a place where the men would let him settle. Ednede and another boy had paired[7], and were going to walk away together when the rains stopped. It was easier for a pair, he said, if their bond was sexual; so long as they offered no competition for women, settled men wouldn't challenge them. But a new man in the region anywhere within three days' walk of an auntring had to prove himself against the settled men there. 'It would 'e three or four years of the sa'e thing,' he said, 'challenging, fighting, always watching the others, on guard[8], showing how strong you are, staying alert all night, all day. To end up living alone your

1 thrum: *(hier) Plätzchen* **2** waken sth.: *(hier) etwas wieder anfachen* **3** crouch: *sich zusammenkauern* **4** snarl: *Zähnefletschen* **5** bare sth.: *etwas freigeben* **6** rags (pl): *Lumpen* **7** pair (v): *ein Paar bilden* **8** on guard: *achtsam*

whole life. I can't do it.' He looked at me. 'I'ne not a 'erson,' he said. 'I want to go ho'e.'

'I'll radio the ship now,' Mother said quietly, with infinite[1] relief.

'No,' I said.

Borny was watching Mother, and raised his hand when she turned to speak to me.

'I'll go,' he said. 'She doesn't have to. Why should she?' Like me, he had learned not to use names without some reason to.

Mother looked from him to me and finally gave a kind of laugh. 'I can't leave her here, Borny!'

'Why should you go?'

'Because I want to,' she said. 'I've had enough. More than enough. We've got a tremendous amount of material on the women, over seven years of it, and now you can fill the information gaps on the men's side. That's enough. It's time, past time, that we all got back to our own people. All of us.'

'I have no people,' I said. 'I don't belong to people. I am trying to be a person. Why do you want to take me away from my soul? You want me to do magic! I won't. I won't do magic. I won't speak your language. I won't go with you!'

My mother was still not listening; she started to answer angrily. Borny put up his hand again, the way a woman does when she is going to sing, and she looked at him.

'We can talk later,' he said. 'We can decide. I need to sleep.'

He hid in our house for two days while we decided what to do and how to do it. That was a miserable time. I stayed home as if I were sick so that I would not lie to the other persons, and Borny and Mother and I talked and talked. Borny asked Mother to stay with me; I asked her to leave me with Sadne or Noyit, either of whom would certainly take me into their household. She refused. She was the mother and I the child and her power was sacred. She radioed the ship and arranged for a lander[2] to pick us up in a barren area

1 infinite: *unendlich* **2** lander: *(hier) Landungsschiff*

two days' walk from the auntring. We left at night, sneaking away[1]. I carried nothing but my soulbag. We walked all next day, slept a little when it stopped raining, walked on and came to the desert. The ground was all lumps[2] and hollows[3] and caves, Before-Time ruins; the soil[4] was tiny bits of glass and hard grains[5] and fragments, the way it is in the deserts. Nothing grew there. We waited there.

The sky broke open and a shining thing fell down and stood before us on the rocks, bigger than any house, though not as big as the ruins of the Before Time. My mother looked at me with a queer, vengeful[6] smile. 'Is it magic?' she said. And it was very hard for me not to think that it was. Yet I knew it was only a thing, and there is no magic in things, only in minds. I said nothing. I had not spoken since we left my home.

I had resolved never to speak to anybody until I got home again; but I was still a child, used to listen and obey. In the ship, that utterly strange new world, I held out only for a few hours, and then began to cry and ask to go home. Please, please, can I go home now.

Everyone on the ship was very kind to me.

Even then I thought about what Borny had been through and what I was going through, comparing our ordeals[7]. The difference seemed total. He had been alone, without food, without shelter, a frightened boy trying to survive among equally frightened rivals against the brutality of older youths intent on having and keeping power, which they saw as manhood. I was cared for, clothed, fed so richly I got sick, kept so warm I felt feverish[8], guided, reasoned with, praised, befriended by citizens of a very great city, offered a share in their power, which they saw as humanity. He and I had both fallen among sorcerors. Both he and I could see the good in the people we were among, but neither he nor I could live with them.

1 sneak away: *sich wegschleichen* **2** lump: *Brocken* **3** hollow: *Loch* **4** soil: *Boden* **5** grain: *Korn* **6** vengeful: *rachsüchtig* **7** ordeal: *Feuerprobe* **8** feverish: *fiebrig*

Borny told me he had spent many desolate nights in the Territory crouched in a fireless shelter[1], telling over the stories he had learned from the aunts, singing the songs in his head. I did the same thing every night on the ship. But I refused to tell the stories or sing to the people there. I would not speak my language, there. It was the only way I had to be silent.

My mother was enraged[2], and for a long time unforgiving[3]. 'You owe your knowledge to our people,' she said. I did not answer, because all I had to say was that they were not my people, that I had no people. I was a person. I had a language that I did not speak. I had my silence. I had nothing else.

I went to school; there were children of different ages on the ship, like an auntring, and many of the adults taught us. I learned Ekumenical history and geography, mostly, and Mother gave me a report to learn about the history of Eleven-Soro, what my language calls the Before Time. I read that the cities of my world had been the greatest cities ever built on any world, covering two of the continents entirely, with small areas set aside for farming, there had been 120 billion[4] people living in the cities, while the animals and the sea and the air and the dirt died, until the people began dying too. It was a hideous[5] story. I was ashamed of it and wished nobody else on the ship or in the Ekumen knew about it. And yet, I thought, if they knew the stories I knew about the Before Time, they would understand how magic turns on itself, and that it must be so.

After less than a year, Mother told us we were going to Hain. The ship's doctor and his clever machines had repaired Borny's lip; he and Mother had put all the information they had into the records; he was old enough to begin training for the Ekumenical Schools, as he wanted to do. I was not flourishing[6], and the doctor's machines were not able to repair me. I kept losing weight, I slept badly, I had terrible headaches. Almost as soon as we came aboard the ship, I

1 shelter: *Unterstand* **2** enraged: angry **3** unforgiving: *unversöhnlich*
4 billion: *Milliarde* **5** hideous: *scheußlich* **6** flourish: *aufblühen, sich entfalten*

had begun to menstruate; each time the cramps were agonizing[1]. 'This is no good, this ship life,' she said. 'You need to be outdoors. On a planet. On a civilized planet.'

'If I went to Hain,' I said, 'when I came back, the persons I know would all be dead hundreds of years ago.'

'Serenity,' she said, 'you must stop thinking in terms of Soro. We have left Soro. You must stop deluding[2] and tormenting[3] yourself, and look forward, not back. Your whole life is ahead of you. Hain is where you will learn to live it."

I summoned up[4] my courage and spoke in my own language: 'I am not a child now. You have no power over me. I will not go. Go without me. You have no power over me!'

Those are the words I had been taught to say to a magician, a sorceror. I don't know if my mother fully understood them, but she did understand that I was deathly afraid of her, and it struck her into silence.

After a long time she said in Hainish, 'I agree. I have no power over you. But I have certain rights; the right of loyalty; of love.'

'Nothing is right that puts me in your power,' I said, still in my language.

She stared at me. 'You are like one of them,' she said. 'You are one of them. You don't know what love is. You're closed into yourself like a rock. I should never have taken you there. People crouching in the ruins of a society – brutal, rigid[5], ignorant, superstitious[6] – each one in a terrible solitude – and I let them make you into one of them!'

'You educated me,' I said, and my voice began to tremble[7] and my mouth to shake around the words, 'and so does the school here, but my aunts educated me, and I want to finish my education.' I was weeping, but I kept standing with my hands clenched[8]. 'I'm not a woman yet. I want to be a woman.'

1 agonizing: *qualvoll* **2** delude sb.: *jdn. täuschen* **3** torment sb.: *jdn. quälen* **4** summon up sth: *etwas aufbringen* **5** rigid: *streng, unbeugsam* **6** superstitious: *abergläubig* **7** tremble: *zittern* **8** clench sth.: *etwas ballen, zusammenpressen*

'But Ren, you will be! – ten times the woman you could ever be on Soro – you must try to understand, to believe me –'

'You have no power over me,' I said, shutting my eyes and putting my hands over my ears. She came to me then and held me, but I stood stiff[1], enduring[2] her touch, until she let me go.

The ship's crew had changed entirely while we were on-planet. The First Observers had gone on to other worlds; our backup was now a Gethenian archeologist named Arrem, a mild, watchful person, not young. Arrem had gone down on-planet only on the two desert continents, and welcomed the chance to talk with us, who had 'lived with the living,' as heshe said. I felt easy when I was with Artera, who was so unlike anybody else. Arrem was not a man – I could not get used to having men around all the time – yet not a woman; and so not exactly an adult, yet not a child: a person, alone, like me. Heshe did not know my language well, but always tried to talk it with me. When this crisis came, Arrem came to my mother and took counsel[3] with her, suggesting that she let me go back down on-planet. Borny was in on some of these talks, and told me about them.

'Arrem says if you go to Hain you'll probably die,' he said. 'Your soul will. Heshe says some of what we learned is like what they learn on Gethen, in their religion. That kind of stopped Mother from ranting about primitive superstition ... And Arrem says you could be useful to the Ekumen, if you stay and finish your education on Soro. You'll be an invaluable resource.' Borny sniggered, and after a minute I did too. 'They'll mine[4] you like an asteroid,' he said. Then he said, 'You know, if you stay and I go, we'll be dead.'

That was how the young people of the ships said it, when one was going to cross the lightyears and the other was going to stay. Goodbye, we're dead. It was the truth.

'I know,' I said. I felt my throat get tight, and was afraid. I had never seen an adult at home cry, except when Sut's baby died. Sut

1 stiff: *steif, erstarrt* **2** endure sth: *etwas ertragen* **3** take counsel: *Rat suchen*
4 mine sth.: take sth. valuable out

howled all night. Howled like a dog, Mother said, but I had never seen or heard a dog, I heard a woman terribly crying. I was afraid of sounding like that. 'If I can go home, when I finish making my soul, who knows, I might come to Hain for a while,' I said, in Hainish.

'Scouting?' Borny said in my language, and laughed, and made me laugh again.

Nobody gets to keep a brother. I knew that. But Borny had come back from being dead to me, so I might come back from being dead to him; at least I could pretend I might.

My mother came to a decision. She and I would stay on the ship for another year while Borny went to Hain. I would keep going to school; if at the end of the year I was still determined to go back on-planet, I could do so. With me or without me, she would go on to Hain then and join Borny. If I ever wanted to see them again, I could follow them. It was a compromise that satisfied no one, but it was the best we could do, and we all consented.

When he left, Borny gave me his knife.

After he left, I tried not to be sick. I worked hard at learning everything they taught me in the ship school, and I tried to teach Arrem how to be aware and how to avoid witchcraft. We did slow walking together in the ship's garden, and the first hour of the untrance movements from the Handdata of Karhide on Gethen. We agreed that they were alike.

The ship was staying in the Soro system not only because of my family, but because the crew was now mostly zoologists who had come to study a sea animal on Eleven-Soro, a kind of cephalopod that had mutated[1] toward high intelligence, or maybe it already was highly intelligent; but there was a communication problem. 'Almost as bad as with the local humans,' said Steadiness, the zoologist who taught and teased us mercilessly. She took us down twice by lander to the uninhabited islands in the Northern Hemisphere where her station was. It was very strange to go down to my world and yet be

1 mutate: *sich verwandeln*

a world away from my aunts and sisters and my soulmate; but I said nothing.

I saw the great, pale, shy creature come slowly up out of the deep waters with a running ripple of colors along its long coiling tentacles and a ringing shimmer of sound, all so quick it was over before you could follow the colors or hear the tune. The zoologist's machine produced a pink glow and a mechanically speeded-up twitter, tinny and feeble in the immensity of the sea. The cephalopod patiently responded in its beautiful silvery shadowy language. 'CP,' Steadiness said to us, ironic – Communication Problem. 'We don't know what we're talking about.'

I said, 'I learned something in my education here. In one of the songs, it says,' and I hesitated, trying to translate it into Hainish, 'it says, thinking is one way of doing and words are one way of thinking.'

Steadiness stared at me, in disapproval I thought, but probably only because I had never said anything to her before except 'Yes'. Finally she said, 'Are you suggesting that it doesn't speak in words?'

'Maybe it's not speaking at all. Maybe it's thinking.'

Steadiness stared at me some more and then said, 'Thank you.' She looked as if she too might be thinking. I wished I could sink into the water, the way the cephalopod was doing.

The other young people on the ship were friendly and mannerly. Those are words that have no translation in my language. I was unfriendly and unmannerly, and they let me be. I was grateful. But there was no place to be alone on the ship. Of course we each had a room; though small, the Heyho was a Hainish-built explorer, designed to give its people room and privacy and comfort and variety and beauty while they hung around in a solar system for years on end. But it was designed. It was all human-made –everything was human. I had much more privacy than I had ever had at home in our one-room house; yet there I had been free and here I was in a trap. I felt the pressure of people all around me, all the time. People around me, people with me, people pressing on me, pressing me to be one of them, to be one of them, one of the people. How could I make my soul? I could barely cling to it. I was in terror that I would lose it altogether.

One of the rocks in my soulbag, a little ugly gray rock that I had picked up on a certain day in a certain place in the hills above the river in the Silver Time, a little piece of my world, that became my world. Every night I took it out and held it in my hand while I lay in bed waiting to sleep, thinking of the sunlight on the hills above the river, listening to the soft hushing[1] of the ship's systems, like a mechanical sea.

The doctor hopefully fed me various tonics[2]. Mother and I ate breakfast together every morning. She kept at work, making our notes from all the years on Eleven-Soro into her report to the Ekumen, but I knew the work did not go well. Her soul was in as much danger as mine was.

'You will never give in, will you, Ren?' she said to me one morning out of the silence of our breakfast. I had not intended the silence as a message. I had only rested in it.

'Mother, I want to go home and you want to go home,' I said. 'Can't we?'

Her expression was strange for a moment, while she misunderstood me; then it cleared to grief, defeat, relief.

'Will we be dead?' she asked me, her mouth twisting.

'I don't know. I have to make my soul. Then I can know if I can come.'

'You know I can't come back. It's up to you.'

'I know. Go see Borny,' I said. 'Go home. Here we're both dying.' Then noises began to come out of me, sobbing[3], howling[4]. Mother was crying. She came to me and held me, and I could hold my mother, cling to her and cry with her, because her spell was broken.

From the lander approaching I saw the oceans of Eleven-Soro, and in the greatness of my joy I thought that when I was grown and went out alone I would go to the sea shore and watch the sea-

1 hushing: calming noise **2** tonic: *Stärkungsmittel* **3** sob: *schluchzen* **4** howl: *heulen, jaulen*

beasts shimmering their colors and tunes till I knew what they were thinking. I would listen, I would learn, till my soul was as large as the shining world. The scarred[1] barrens[2] whirled[3] beneath us, rains as wide as the continent, endless desolations[4]. We touched down. I had my soulbag, and Borny's knife around my neck on its string a communicator implant behind my right earlobe[5], and a medicine kit Mother had made for me. 'No use dying of an infected finger, after all,' she had said. The people on the lander said good-bye, but I forgot to. I set off out of the desert, home.

It was summer; the night was short and warm; I walked most of it. I got to the auntring about the middle of the second day. I went to my house cautiously[6], in case somebody had moved in while I was gone; but it was just as we had left it. The mattresses were moldy, and I put them and the bedding out in the sun, and started going over the garden to see what had kept growing by itself. The pigi had got small and seedy[7], but there were some good roots. A little boy came by and stared; he had to be Migi's baby. After a while Hyuru came by. She squatted down[8] near me in the garden in the sunshine. I smiled when I saw her, and she smiled, but it took us a while to find something to say.

'Your mother didn't come back,' she said.

'She's dead,' I said.

'I'm sorry,' Hyuru said.

She watched me dig up another root.

'Will you come to the singing circle?' she asked.

I nodded.

She smiled again. With her rosebrown skin and wide-set eyes, Hyuru had become very beautiful, but her smile was exactly the same as when we were little girls. 'Hi, ya!' she sighed in deep contentment, lying down on the dirt with her chin on her arms. 'This is good!'

1 scarred: *vernarbt* **2** barrens: *(hier) ödes Land* **3** whirl: *wirbeln* **4** desolation: *Verwüstung* **5** earlobe: *Ohrläppchen* **6** cautiously: *vorsichtig* **7** seedy: *heruntergekommen, verwahrlost* **8** squat down: *sich hinhocken*

I went on blissfully digging.

That year and the next two, I was in the singing circle with Hyuru and two other girls. Didsu still came to it often, and Han, a woman who settled in our auntring to have her first baby, joined it too. In the singing circle the older girls pass around the stories, songs, knowledge they learned from their own mother, and young women who have lived in other auntrings teach what they learned there; so women make each other's souls, learning how to make their children's souls.

Han lived in the house where old Dnemi had died. Nobody in the auntring except Sut's baby had died while my family lived there. My mother had complained that she didn't have any data on death and burial[1]. Sut had gone away with her dead baby and never came back, and nobody talked about it. I think that turned my mother against the others more than anything else. She was angry and ashamed that she could not go and try to comfort Sut and that nobody else did. 'It is not human,' she said. 'It is pure animal behavior. Nothing could be clearer evidence that this is a broken culture – not a society, but the remains of one. A terrible, an appalling poverty.'

I don't know if Dnemi's death would have changed her mind. Dnemi was dying for a long time, of kidney failure I think; she turned a kind of dark orange color, jaundice. While she could get around, nobody helped her. When she didn't come out of her house for a day or two, the women would send the children in with water and a little food and firewood. It went on so through the winter; then one morning little Rashi told his mother Aunt Dnemi was 'staring'. Several of the women went to Dnemi's house, and entered it for the first and last time. They sent for all the girls in the singing circle, so that we could learn what to do. We took turns sitting by the body or in the porch[2] of the house, singing soft songs, child-songs, giving the soul a day and a night to leave the body and the house; then the older women wrapped[3] the body in the bedding[4], strapped it on a

1 burial: *Bestattung* **2** porch: *Veranda* **3** wrap sth.: *etwas einwickeln*
4 bedding: *Bettwäsche*

kind of litter[1], and set off with it toward the barren[2] lands. There it would be given back, under a rock cairn[3] or inside one of the ruins of the ancient city. 'Those are the lands of the dead,' Sadne said. 'What dies stays there.'

Hah settled down in that house a year later. When her baby began to be born she asked Didsu to help her, and Hyuru and I stayed in the porch and watched, so that we could learn. It was a wonderful thing to see, and quite altered the course of my thinking, and Hyuru's too. Hyuru said, 'I'd like to do that!' I said nothing, but thought, So do I, but not for a long time, because once you have a child you're never alone.

And though it is of the others, of relationships, that I write, the heart of my life has been my being alone.

I think there is no way to write about being alone. To write is to tell something to somebody, to communicate to others. CP, as Steadiness would say. Solitude is non-communication, the absence of others, the presence of a self sufficient to itself.

A woman's solitude in the auntring is, of course, based firmly on the presence of others at a little distance. It is a contingent, and therefore human, solitude. The settled men are connected as stringently to the women, though not to one another; the settlement is an integral though distant element of the auntring. Even a scouting woman is part of the society – a moving part, connecting the settled parts. Only the isolation of a woman or man who chooses to live outside the settlements is absolute. They are outside the network altogether. There are worlds where such persons are called saints, holy people. Since isolation is a sure way to prevent magic, on my world the assumption is that they are sorcerors, outcast by others or by their own will, their conscience[4].

I knew I was strong with magic, how could I help it? and I began to long to get away. It would be so much easier and safer to be alone. But at the same time, and increasingly, I wanted to know something

1 litter: *Trage* **2** barren: *karg, öde* **3** cairn: *Hügel, Haufen* **4** conscience: *Bewusstsein*

about the great harmless magic, the spells cast between men and women.

I preferred foraging to gardening, and was out on the hills a good deal; and these days, instead of keeping away from the man's-houses, I wandered by them, and looked at them, and looked at the men if they were outside. The men looked back. Downriver Lame Man's long, shining hair was getting a little white in it now, but when he sat singing his long, long songs I found myself sitting down and listening, as if my legs had lost their bones. He was very handsome. So was the man I remembered as a boy named Tret in the auntring, when I was little, Behyu's son. He had come back from the boygroup and from wandering, and had built a house and made a fine garden in the valley of Red Stone Creek. He had a big nose and big eyes, long arms and legs, long hands; he moved very quietly, almost like Arrem doing the untrance. I went often to pick lowberries in Red Stone Creek valley.

He came along the path and spoke. 'You were Borny's sister,' he said. He had a low voice, quiet.

'He's dead,' I said.

Red Stone Man nodded. 'That's his knife.'

In my world, I had never talked with a man. I felt extremely strange. I kept picking berries.

'You're picking green ones,' Red Stone Man said.

His soft, smiling voice made my legs lose their bones again.

'I think nobody's touched you,' he said. 'I'd touch you gently. I think about it, about you, ever since you came by here early in the summer. Look, here's a bush full of ripe ones. Those are green. Come over here.'

I came closer to him, to the bush of ripe berries.

When I was on the ship, Arrem told me that many languages have a single word for sexual desire and the bond between mother and child and the bond between soulmates and the feeling for one's home and worship of the sacred[1]; they are all called love. There

1 the sacred (n): *das Heilige*

is no word that great in my language. Maybe my mother is right, and human greatness perished in my world with the people of the Before Time, leaving only small, poor, broken things and thoughts. In my language, love is many different words. I learned one of them with Red Stone Man. We sang it together to each other.

We made a brush house on a little cove of the creek, and neglected our gardens, but gathered many, many sweet berries.

Mother had put a lifetime's worth of nonconceptives[1] in the little medicine kit. She had no faith in Sorovian herbals. I did, and they worked.

But when a year or so later, in the Golden Time, I decided to go out scouting, I thought I might go places where the right herbs were scarce; and so I stuck the little noncon jewel on the back of my left earlobe. Then I wished I hadn't, because it seemed like witchcraft. Then I told myself I was being superstitious; the noncon wasn't any more witchcraft than the herbs were, it just worked longer. I had promised my mother in my soul that I would never be superstitious. The skin grew over the noncon, and I took my soulbag and Borny's knife and the medicine kit, and set off across the world.

I had told Hyuru and Red Stone Man I would be leaving. Hyuru and I sang and talked together all one night down by the river. Red Stone Man said in his soft voice, 'Why do you want to go?' and I said, 'To get away from your magic, sorcerer,' which was true in part. If I kept going to him I might always go to him. I wanted to give my soul and body a larger world to be in.

Now to tell of my scouting years is more difficult than ever. CP! A woman scouting is entirely alone, unless she chooses to ask a settled man for sex, or camps in an auntring for a while to sing and listen with the singing circle. If she goes anywhere near the territory of a boygroup, she is in danger; and if she comes on a rogue she is in danger; and if she hurts herself or gets into polluted country, she is in danger. She has no responsibility except to herself, and so much freedom is very dangerous.

1 nonconceptive: *(hier) Verhütungsmittel*

In my right earlobe was the tiny communicator; every forty days, as I had promised, I sent a signal to the ship that meant 'all well'. If I wanted to leave, I would send another signal. I could have called for the lander to rescue me from a bad situation, but though I was in bad situations a couple of times I never thought of using it. My signal was the mere[1] fulfillment[2] of a promise to my mother and her people, the network I was no longer part of, a meaningless communication.

Life in the auntring, or for a settled man, is repetitive, as I said; and so it can be dull. Nothing new happens. The mind always wants new happenings. So for the young soul there is wandering and scouting, travel, danger, change. But of course travel and danger and change have their own dullness. It is finally always the same otherness over again; another hill, another river, another man, another day. The feet begin to turn in a long, long circle. The body begins to think of what it learned back home, when it learned to be still. To be aware. To be aware of the grain of dust beneath the sole of the foot, and the skin of the sole of the foot, and the touch and scent[3] of the air on the cheek, and the fall and motion of the light across the air, and the color of the grass on the high hill across the river, and the thoughts of the body, of the soul, the shimmer[4] and ripple[5] of colors and sounds in the clear darkness of the depths, endlessly moving, endlessly changing, endlessly new.

So at last I came back home. I had been gone about four years.

Hyuru had moved into my old house when she left her mother's house. She had not gone scouting, but had taken to going to Red Stone Creek Valley; and she was pregnant. I was glad to see her living there. The only house empty was an old half-ruined one too close to Hedimi's. I decided to make a new house. I dug out the circle as deep as my chest; the digging took most of the summer. I cut the sticks, braced[6] and wove them, and then daubed[7] the framework solidly

1 mere: *bloß* **2** fulfillment: *Erfüllung* **3** scent: *Geruch* **4** shimmer: *Schillern* **5** ripple: *Welligkeit* **6** brace sth.: *etwas festigen* **7** daub sth.: *etwas verputzen, etwas bewerfen*

with mud inside and out. I remembered when I had done that with my mother long long ago, and how she had said, 'That's right. That's good.' I left the roof open, and the hot sun of late summer baked the mud into clay[1]. Before the rains came, I thatched[2] the house with reeds, a triple thatching, for I'd had enough of being wet all winter.

My auntring was more a string[3] than a ring stretching along the north bank of the river for about three kilos; my house lengthened the string a good bit, upstream from all the others. I could just see the smoke from Hyuru's fireplace. I dug it into a sunny slope[4] with good drainage[5]. It is still a good house.

I settled down. Some of my time went to gathering and gardening and mending[6] and all the dull[7], repetitive[8] actions of primitive life, and some went to singing and thinking the songs and stories I had learned here at home and while scouting and the things I had learned on the ship, also. Soon enough I found why women are glad to have children come to listen to them, for songs and stories are meant to be heard, listened to. 'Listen!' I would say to the children. The children of the auntring came and went, like the little fish in the river, one or two or five of them, little ones, big ones. When they came, I sang or told stories to them. When they left, I went on in silence. Sometimes I joined the singing circle to give what I had learned traveling to the older girls. And that was all I did; except that I worked, always, to be aware of all I did.

By solitude the soul escapes from doing or suffering[9] magic; it escapes from dullness, from boredom, by being aware. Nothing is boring if you are aware of it. It may be irritating but it is not boring. If it is pleasant the pleasure will not fail so long as you are aware of it. Being aware is the hardest work the soul can do, I think.

I helped Hyuru have her baby, a girl, and played with the baby. Then after a couple of years I took the noncon out of my left earlobe. Since it left a little hole, I made the hole go all the way through with

1 clay: *Ton* **2** thatch sth.: *etwas mit Stroh decken* **3** string: *Reihe* **4** slope: *Abhang* **5** drainage: *Abfluss* **6** mend: *ausbessern* **7** dull: boring **8** repetitive: *sich wiederholend* **9** suffer sth.: *etwas erleiden*

a burnt needle, and when it healed I hung in it a tiny jewel I had found in a rain when I was scouting. I had seen a man on the ship with a jewel hung in his ear that way. I wore it when I went out foraging. I kept clear of Red Stone Valley. The man there behaved as if he had a claim on me, a right to me. I liked him still, but I did not like that smell of magic about him, his imagination of power over me. I went up into the hills, northward.

A pair of young men had settled in old North House about the time I came home. Often boys got through boygroup by pairing, and often they stayed paired when they left the Territory. It helped their chances of survival. Some of them were sexually paired, others weren't; some stayed paired, others didn't. One of this pair had gone off with another man last summer. The one that stayed wasn't a handsome man, but I had noticed him. He had a kind of solidness I liked. His body and hands were short and strong. I had courted him a little, but he was very shy. This day, a day in the Silver Time when the mist lay on the river, he saw the jewel swinging in my ear, and his eyes widened.

'It's pretty, isn't it?' I said.

He nodded.

'I wore it to make you look at me,' I said.

He was so shy that I finally said, 'If you only like sex with men, you know, just tell me.' I really was not sure.

'Oh, no,' he said, 'no. No.' He stammered[1] and then bolted[2] back down the path. But he looked back; and I followed him slowly, still not certain whether he wanted me or wanted to be rid of me.

He waited for me in front of a little house in a grove of redroot[3], a lovely little bower[4], all leaves outside, so that you would walk within arm's length of it and not see it. Inside he had laid sweet grass, deep and dry and soft, smelling of summer. I went in, crawling because the door was very low, and sat in the summer-smelling grass. He stood outside. 'Come in,' I said, and he came in very slowly.

'I made it for you,' he said.

1 stammer: *stottern* **2** bolt: *eilen* **3** redroot: *Fuchsschwanz* **4** bower: *Laube*

'Now make a child for me,' I said.

And we did that; maybe that day, maybe another.

Now I will tell you why after all these years I called the ship, not knowing even if it was still there in the space between the planets, asking for the lander to meet me in the barren land.

When my daughter was born, that was my heart's desire and the fulfillment of my soul. When my son was born, last year, I knew there is no fulfillment. He will grow toward manhood, and go, and fight and endure[1], and live or die as a man must. My daughter, whose name is Yedneke, Leaf, like my mother, will grow to womanhood and go or stay as she chooses. I will live alone. This is as it should be, and my desire. But I am of two worlds; I am a person of this world, and a woman of my mother's people. I owe my knowledge to the children of her people. So I asked the lander to come, and spoke to the people on it. They gave me my mother's report to read, and I have written my story in their machine, making a record for those who want to learn one of the ways to make a soul. To them, to the children I say: Listen! Avoid magic! Be aware!

1 endure: *durchstehen*

Peter Phillips

Lost Memory

Peter Phillips (1920–2012) was a British journalist and author of science fiction short stories. All his short stories were published between 1948 and the mid-1950s, when Phillips decided to retire from writing. Phillips was mainly interested in exploring the concept of mind control and the effects of long-time space travel in his fiction. During his short creative period of only nine years, Phillips published 21 short stories but is nevertheless considered one of the most influential science-fiction authors of the 20th century, especially due to his exceptional ability to blur the boundaries between science fiction and fantasy.

Imagine a robot society without any human beings. What would it look like? Speculate about what may have happened to the humans. Consider how a robot might react if it discovered a human being for the first time.

I collapsed joints[1] and hung up to talk with Dak-whirr. He blinked his eyes in some discomfort.

'What do you want, Palil?' he asked complainingly.

'As if you didn't know.'

'I can't give you permission to examine it. The thing is being saved for inspection by the board. What guarantee do I have that you won't spoil it for them?'

I thrust[2] confidentially at one of his body-plates. 'You owe me a favour,' I said. 'Remember'?'

'That was a long time in the past.'

'Only two thousand revolutions and a reassembly[3] ago. If it wasn't for me, you'd be eroding[4] in a pit. All I want is a quick look at

1 joints (pl): *Gelenke, Scharniere* **2** thrust at sb./sth.: *an jdm./etwas stoßen*
3 reassembly: *Wiedermontage* **4** erode: dissolve

its thinking part. I'll vrull the consciousness without laying a single pair of pliers[1] on it.'

He went into a feedback twitch[2], an indication of the conflict between his debt to me and his self-conceived duty.

Finally he said, 'Very well, but keep tuned to me. If I warn that a board member is coming, remove yourself quickly. Anyway how do you know it has consciousness? It may be mere primal metal.'

'In that form? Don't be foolish. It's obviously a manufacture. And I'm not conceited[3] enough to believe that we are the only form of intelligent manufacture in the Universe.'

'Tautologous[4] phrasing, Palil,' Dak-whirr said pedantically. 'There could not conceivably be "unintelligent manufacture". There can be no consciousness without manufacture, and no manufacture without intelligence. Now if you should wish to dispute –'

I tuned off his frequency abruptly and hurried away. Dak-whirr is a fool and a bore. Everyone knows there's a fault in his logic circuit, but he refuses to have it traced down and repaired. Very unintelligent of him.

The things had been taken into one of the museum sheds by the carriers. I gazed at it in admiration for some moments. It was quite beautiful, having suffered only slight exterior damage, and it was obviously no mere conglomeration[5] of sky metal.

In fact, I immediately thought of it as 'he' and endowed it with the attributes of self-knowing, although, of course, his consciousness could not be functioning or he would have attempted communication with us.

I fervently hoped that the board, after his careful disassembly and study, could restore his awareness so that he could tell us himself which solar system he came from.

Imagine it! He had achieved our dream of many thousands of revolutions – space flight – only to be fused, or worse, in his moment of triumph.

1 pliers (pl): *Zange* **2** twitch: *Zucken* **3** conceited: *arrogant* **4** tautologous: saying the same thing twice **5** conglomeration: collection

I felt a surge of sympathy for the lonely traveller as he lay there, still, silent, non-emitting. Anyway, I mused, even if we couldn't restore him to self-knowing, an analysis of his construction might give us the secret of the power he had used to achieve the velocity[1] to escape his planet's gravity.

In shape and size he was not unlike Swen – or Swen Two, as he called himself after his conversion – who failed so disastrously to reach our satellite, using chemical fuels. But where Swen Two had placed his tubes, the stranger had curious helical[2] construction studded[3] at irregular intervals with small crystals.

He was thirty-five feet tall, a gracefully tapering cylinder. Standing at his head, I could find no sign of exterior vision cells, so I assumed he had some kind of vrulling sense. There seemed to be no exterior markings at all, except the long, shallow grooves[4] dented in his skin by scraping to a stop along the hard surface of our planet.

I am a reporter with warm current in my wires, not a cold-thinking scientist, so I hesitated before using my own vrulling sense. Even though the stranger was non-aware – perhaps permanently – I felt it would be a presumption[5], an invasion of privacy. There was nothing else I could do, though, of course.

I started to vrull, gently at first, then harder, until I was positively glowing with effort. It was incredible; his skin seemed absolutely impermeable.

The sudden realization that metal could be so alien nearly fused something inside me. I found myself backing away in horror, my self-preservation relay working overtime.

Imagine watching one of the beautiful cone-rod-and-cylinder assemblies performing the Dance of the Seven Spanners[6], as he's conditioned to do, and then suddenly refusing to do anything except stump around unattractively, or even becoming obstinately motionless, unresponsive. That might give you an idea of how I felt in that dreadful moment.

1 velocity: speed **2** helical: *spiralförmig* **3** stud sth.: *etwas besetzen* **4** groove: *Furche, Nut* **5** presumption: *Dreistigkeit* **6** spanner: *Schraubenschlüssel*

Then I remembered Dak-whirr's words – there could be no such thing as an 'unintelligent manufacture.' And a product so beautiful could surely not be evil. I overcame my repugnance[1] and approached again.

I halted as an open transmission came from someone near at hand.

'Who gave that squeaking reporter permission to snoop around[2] here?'

I had forgotten the museum board. Five of them were standing in the doorway of the shed, radiating anger. I recognized Chirik, the chairman, and addressed myself to him. I explained that I'd interfered with nothing and pleaded for permission on behalf of my subscribers to watch their investigation of the stranger. After some argument, they allowed me to stay.

I watched in silence and some amusement as one by one they tried to vrull the silent being from space. Each showed the same reaction as I had when they failed to penetrate the skin.

Chirik, who is wheeled – and inordinately vain about his suspension system – flung himself back on his supports and pretended to be thinking.

'Fetch Fiff-Fiff,' he said at last. 'The creature may still be aware, but unable to communicate on our standard frequencies.'

Fiff-fiff can detect anything in any spectrum. Fortunately he was at work in the museum that day and soon arrived in answer to the call. He stood silently near the stranger for some moments, testing and adjusting himself, then slid up the electromagnetic band.

'He's emitting,' he said.

'Why can't we get him?' asked Chirik.

'It's a curious signal on an unusual band.'

'Well, what does he say?'

'Sounds like utter nonsense to me. Wait, I'll relay and convert it to standard.'

1 repugnance: *Widerwille* **2** snoop around: *herumschnüffeln*

I made a direct recording naturally, like any good reporter.

'– after planetfall,' the stranger was saying. 'Last dribble of power. If you don't pick this up, my name is Entropy. Other instruments knocked to hell, airlock[1] jammed[2] and I'm too weak to open it manually. Becoming delirious, too, I guess. Getting strong undirectional ultra-wave reception in Inglish, craziest stuff you ever heard, like goblins[3] muttering, and I know we were the only ship in this sector. If you pick this up, but can't get a fix in time, give my love to the boys in the mess. Signing off for another couple of hours, but keeping this channel open and hoping …'

'The fall must have deranged[4] him,' said Chirik, gazing at the stranger. 'Can't he see us or hear us?'

'He couldn't hear you properly before, but he can now, through me,' Fiff-fiff pointed out. 'Say something to him, Chirik.'

'Hello,' said Chrirk doubtfully. 'Er– welcome to our planet. We are sorry you were hurt by your fall. We offer you the hospitality of our assembly shops. You will feel better when you are repaired and repowered. If you will indicate how we can assist you –'

'What the hell! What ship is that? Where are you?'

'We're here,' said Chirik. 'Can't you see us or vrull us? Your vision circuit is impaired[5], perhaps? Or do you depend entirely on vrulling? We can't find your eyes and assumed either that you protected them in some way during flight, or dispensed with vision cells altogether in your conversion.'

Chirik hesitated, continued apologetically: 'But we cannot understand how you vrull, either. While we thought that you were unaware, or even completely fused, we tried to vrull you. Your skin is quite impervious[6] to us, however.'

The stranger said: 'I don't know if you're batty[7] or I am. What distance are you from me?'

1 airlock: *Luftschleuse* **2** jammed: blocked **3** goblin: *Kobold* **4** derange sb.: make sb. confused or mad **5** impaired: damaged **6** impervious: *umempfindlich* **7** batty: *verrückt*

Chirik measured quickly. 'One meter, two-point-five centimetres from my eyes to your nearest point. Within touching distance, in fact.' Chirik tentatively put out his hand. 'Can you not feel me, or has your contact sense also been affected?'

It became obvious that the stranger had been pitifully deranged. I reproduce his words phonetically from my record, although some of them make little sense. Emphasis, punctuative pauses and spelling of unknown terms are mere guesswork, of course.

He said: 'For godsakeman stop talking nonsense, whoever you are. If you're outside, can't you see the airlock is jammed? Can't shift it myself. I'm badly hurt. Get me out of here, please.'

'Get you out of where?' Chirik looked around, puzzled. 'We brought you into an open shed near our museum for a preliminary examination. Now that we know you're intelligent, we shall immediately take you to our assembly shops for healing and recuperation. Rest assured that you'll have the best possible attention.'

There was a lengthy pause before the stranger spoke again, and his words were slow and deliberate. His bewilderment is understandable, I believe, if we remember that he could not see, vrull or feel.

He asked: 'What manner of creature are you? Describe yourself.'

Chirik turned to us and made a significant gesture toward his thinking part, indicating gently that the injured stranger had to be humored.

'Certainly,' he replied. 'I am an unspecialized bipedal[1] manufacture of standard proportions, lately self-converted to wheeled traction, with a hydraulic suspension system of my own devising which I'm sure will interest you when we restore your sense circuits.'

There was an even longer silence.

'You are robots,' the stranger said at last. 'Crise[2] knows how you got here or why you speak Inglish, but you must try to understand

1 bipedal: *zweibeinig* **2** Chrise: *Christ*

me. I am mann. I am a friend of your master, your maker. You must fetch him to me at once.'

'You are not well,' said Chirik firmly. 'Your speech is incoherent[1] and without meaning. Your fall has obviously caused several serious feedbacks of a very serious nature. Please lower your voltage. We are taking you to our shops immediately. Reserve your strength to assist our specialists as best you can in diagnosing your troubles.'

'Wait. You must understand. You are – ogodno[2] that's no good. Have you no memory of mann? The words you use – what meaning have they for you? Manufacture – made by hand hand hand darnyou. Healing. Metal is not healed. Skin. Skin is not metal. Eyes. Eyes are not scanning cells. Eyes grow. Eyes are soft. My eyes are soft. Mine eyes have seen the glory – steady on, sun. Get a grip. Take it easy. You out there listen.'

'Out where?' asked Prr-chuck, deputy chairman of the museum board.

I shook my head sorrowfully. This was nonsense, but, like any good reporter, I kept my recorder running.

The mad words flowed on. 'You call me he. Why? You have no seks. You are knewter. You are it it it! I am he, he who made you, sprung from shee, born of wumman. What is wumman, who is silv-ya what is shee that all her swains commend her[3] ogod the bluds flowing again. Remember. Think back, you out there. These words were made by mann, for mann. Hurt, healing, hospitality, horror, deth by loss of blud. Deth. Blud. Do you understand these words? Do you remember the soft things that made you? Soft little mann who konkurred[4] the Galaxy and made sentient[5] slaves of his machines and saw the wonders of a million worlds, only this miserable representative has to die in lonely desperation on a far planet, hearing goblin voices in the darkness.'

1 incoherent: *zusammenhanglos* **2** ogodno: Oh God, no! **3** Who is Silvia? what is she, That all our swains commend her?: line from Shakespeare's *Two Gentlemen of Verona;* swain: lover **4** konkurred: conquered **5** sentient: having the use of the five senses

Here my recorder reproduces a most curious sound, as though the stranger were using an ancient type of vibratory molecular vocalize in a gaseous medium to reproduce his words before transmission, and the insulation[1] on his diaphragm[2] had come adrift.

It was a jerky, high-pitched, strangely disturbing sound; but in a moment the fault was corrected and the stranger resumed transmission.

'Does blud mean anything to you?'

'No,' Chirik replied simply.

'Or deth?'

'No.'

'Or wor[3]?'

'Quite meaningless.'

'What is your origin? How did you come into being?'

'There are several theories,' Chirik said. 'The most popular one – which is no more than a grossly unscientific legend, in my opinion – is that our manufacturer fell from the skies, imbedded in a mass of primal metal on which He drew to erect the first assembly shop. How He came into being is left to conjecture. My own theory, however – '

'Does legend mention the shape of this primal metal?'

'In vague terms, yes. It was cylindrical, of vast dimensions.'

'An interstellar vessel,' said the stranger.

'That is my view also,' said Chrik complacently. 'And – '

'What was the supposed appearance of your – manufacturer?'

'He is said to have been of magnificent proportions, based harmoniously on a cubical plan, static in Himself, but equipped with a vast array[4] of senses.'

'An automatic computer,' said the stranger.

He made more curious noises, less jerky and at a lower pitch than the previous sounds.

He corrected the fault and went on: 'God that's funny. A ship falls, men are no more and an automatic computer has pupps[5]. Oh,

1 insulation: *Isolierung* **2** diaphragm: *Zwerchfell* **3** wor: war **4** array: *Palette*
5 pupp = pup: (here) child

yes, it fits in. A self-setting computer and navigator, operating on verbal orders. It learns to listen for itself and know itself for what it is, and to absorb knowledge. It comes to hate men – or at least their bad qualities – so it deliberately crashes the ship and pulps their puny bodies with a calculated nicety of shock. Then it propagates and does a dam fine job of selective erasure[1] on whatever it gave its pupps to use for memory. It passes on only the good it found in menn, and purges the memory of him completely. Even purges all of his vocabulary except scientific terminology. Oil is thicker than blud. Soo may they live without the burden of knowing that they are – ogod they must know, they must understand. You outside, what happened to this manufacturer?'

Chirik, despite his professed disbelief in the supernormal aspects of the ancient story, automatically made a visual sign of sorrow.

'Legend has it,' he said, 'that after completing His task, He fused[2] himself beyond possibility of healing.'

Abrupt, low-pitched noises came again from the stranger. 'Yes. He would. Just in case any of His pupps should give themselves forbidden knowledge and an infeeryorrity komplecks by probing his mnemonic circuits. The perfect self-sacrificing muther. What sort of environment did He give you? Describe your planet.'

Chrik looked around at us again in bewilderment, but he replied courteously, giving the stranger a description of our world.

'Of course,' said the stranger. 'Of course. Sterile rock and metal suitable only for you. But there must be some way ...'

He was silent for a while.

'Do you know what growth means?' he asked finally. 'Do you have anything that grows?'

'Certainly,' Chirik said helpfully. 'If we should suspend a crystal of some substance in a saturated solution of the same element or compound –'

1 erasure: removal **2** fuse: *schmelzen*

'No, no,' the stranger interrupted. 'Have you nothing that grows of itself, that fruktiffies and gives increase without your intervention?'

'How could such a thing be?'

'Crisellmytee[1] I should have guessed. If you had one blade of gras, just one tiny blade of growing gras, you could extrapolate from that to me. Green things, things that feed on the rich brest of erth, cells that divide and multiply, a cool grove of treez in a hot summer, with tiny warmbludded burds preening[2] their fethers among the leeves; a feeld of spring weet with newbawn mise timidly threading the dangerous jungul of stroks; a stream of living water where silver fish dart and pry[3] and feed and procreate; a farm yard where things grunt and cluck and greet the new day with the stirring pulse of life, with a surge of blud. Blud –'

For some inexplicable reason, although the strength of his carrier wave remained almost constant, the stranger's transmission seemed to be growing fainter.

'His circuits are failing,' Chirik said. 'Call the carriers. We must take him to an assembly shop immediately. I wish he would reserve his power.'

My presence with the museum board was accepted without question now. I hurried along with them as the stranger was carried to the nearest shop.

I now noticed a circular marking in that part of his skin on which he had been resting, and guessed that it was some kind of orifice[4] through which he would have extended his planetary traction mechanism if he had not been injured.

He was gently placed on a disassembly cradle[5]. The doctor in charge that day was Chur-chur, an old friend of mine. He had been listening to the two-way transmission and was already acquainted with the case.

Chur-chur walked thoughtfully around the stranger.

1 Crisellmytee: Christ Almighty **2** preen sth.: (of a bird) clean sth. **3** pry: *schnüffeln* **4** orifice: *Öffnung* **5** cradle: *Hängebühne*

'We shall have to cut,' he said. 'It won't pain him, since his intra-molecular pressure and contact senses have failed. But since we can't vrull him, it'll be necessary for him to tell us where his main brain is housed or we might damage it.'

Fiff-fiff was still relaying, but no amount of power boost would make the stranger's voice any clearer. It was quite faint now, and there are places on my recorder tape from which I cannot make even the roughest phonetic transliteration[1].

'... strength going. Can't get into my zoot ... done for if they bust through lock, done for if they don't ... must tell them I need oxygen ...'

'He's in bad shape, desirous of extinction.' I remarked to Chur-chur, who was adjusting his arc-cutter. 'He wants to poison himself with oxidation now.'

I shuddered at the thought of that vile[2], corrosive gas he had mentioned, which causes that almost unmentionable condition we all fear – rust.

Chirik spoke firmly through Fiff-fiff. 'Where is your thinking part, stranger? Your central brain?'

'In my head,' the stranger replied. 'In my head ogod my head... eyes blurring everything going dim ... luv to mairee ... kids ... a carry me home to the lone prayree[3] ... get this bluddy airlock open then they'll see me die ... but they'll see me ... some kind of atmosphere with this gravity ... se me die ... extrapolate from body what I was ... what they are damthem damthem damthem ... mann ... master ... I AM YOUR MAKER!'

For a few seconds the voice rose strong and clear, then faded away again and dwindled into a combination of those two curious noises I mentioned earlier. For some reason that I cannot explain. I found the combined sound very disturbing despite its faintness. It may be that it included some kind of sympathetic oscillation[4].

1 phonetic transliteration: *lautliche Umschrift* **2** vile: *scheußlich* **3** carry me home to the lone prairie: cowboy song about dying **4** oscillation: *Schwingung*

Then came words, largely incoherent and punctuated by a kind of surge like the sonic vibrations produced by variations of pressure in a leaking gas-filled vessel.

'... done it ... crawling into chamber, closing inner ... must be mad... they'd find me anyway ... but finished ... want see them before I die... want see them see me ... liv few seconds, watch them ... get outer one open ...'

Chur-chur had adjusted his arc to a broad, clean, blue-white glare. I trembled a little as he brought it near the edge of the circular marking in the stranger's skin. I could almost feel the disruption of the intra-molecular sense currents in my own skin.

'Don't be squeamish[1], Palil,' Chur-chur said kindly. 'He can't feel it now that his contact sense has gone. And you heard him say that his central brain is in his head.' He brought the cutter firmly up to the skin. 'I should have guessed that. He's the same shape as Swen Two, and Swen very logically concentrated his main thinking part as far away from his explosion chambers as possible.'

Rivulets[2] of metal ran down into a tray which a calm assistant had placed on the ground for that purpose. I averted my eyes quickly. I could never steel myself enough to be a surgical engineer or assembly technician.

But I had to look again, fascinated. The whole area circumscribed by the marking was beginning to glow.

Abruptly the stranger's voice returned, quite strongly, each word clipped, emphasized, high-pitched.

'Ar no no no ... god my hands ... they're burning through the lock and I can't get back I can't get away ... stop it you feens stop it can't you hear ... I'll be burned to deth I'm here in the airlock ... the air's getting hot you're burning me alive ...'

Although the words made little sense, I could guess what had happened and I was horrified.

1 squeamish: *zimperlich* **2** rivulet: *Bach*

'Stop, Chur-chur,' I pleaded. 'The heat has somehow brought back his skin currents. It's hurting him.'

Chur-chur said reassuringly: 'Sorry, Palil. It occasionally happens during an operation – probably a local thermo-electric effect. But even if his contact senses have started working again and he can't switch them off, he won't have to bear this very long.'

Chirik shared my unease, however. He put out his hand and awkwardly patted the stranger's skin.

'Easy there,' he said. 'Cut out your senses if you can. If you can't, well, the operation is nearly finished. Then we'll repower you, and you'll soon be fit and happy again, healed and fitted and reassembled.'

I decided that I liked Chirik very much just then. He exhibited almost as much self-induced empathy as any reporter; he might even come to like my favourite blue stars, despite his cold scientific exactitude in most respects.

My recorder tape shows, in its reproduction of certain sounds, how I was torn away from this strained reverie.

During the one-and-a-half seconds I had recorded the distinct vocables 'burning me alive,' the stranger's words had become quite blurred, running together and rising even higher in pitch until they reached a sustained note – around E-flat in the standard sonic scale.

It was not like a voice at all.

This high, whining[1] noise was suddenly modulated by apparent words, but without changing its pitch. Transcribing what seem to be words is almost impossible, as you can see for yourself – this is the closest I can come phonetically:

'Eeee ahahmbeeeing baked alive in an uvennn ahdeeer-jee-sussunmuuutherrr!'

The note swooped higher and higher until it must have neared supersonic range, almost beyond either my direct or recorded hearing.

Then it stopped as quickly as a contact break.

1 whining: *wimmernd*

And although the soft hiss of the stranger's carrier wave carried on without perceptible diminution, indicating that some degree of awareness still existed, I experienced at that moment one of those quirks of intuition given only to reporters.

I felt that I would never greet the beautiful stranger from the sky in his full senses.

Chur-chur was muttering to himself about the extreme toughness and thickness of the stranger's skin. He has to make four complete cutting revolutions before the circular mass of nearly white-hot metal could be pulled away by a magnetic-grapple.

A billow of smoke puffed out of the orifice. Despite my repugnance, I thought of my duty as a reporter and forced myself to look over Chur-hur's shoulder.

The fumes came from a soft, charred, curiously shaped mass of something which lay just inside the opening.

'Undoubtedly a kind of insulating material,' Chur-chur explained.

He drew out the crumpled blackish heap and placed it carefully on a tray. A small portion broke away, showing a red, viscid substance.

'It looks complex,' Chur-chur said, 'but I expect the stranger will be able to tell us how to reconstitute it or make a substitute.'

His assistant gently cleaned the wound of the remainder of the material, which he placed with the rest; and Chur-chur resumed his inspection of the orifice.

You can, if you want, read the technical accounts of Chur-chur's discovery of the stranger's double skin at the point where the cut was made; of the incredible complexity of his driving mechanism, involving principles which are still not understood to this day; of the museum's failure to analyze the exact nature and function of the insulating material found in only that one portion of his body; and of the other scientific mysteries connected with him.

But this is my personal, non-scientific account. I shall never forget hearing about the greatest mystery of all, for which not even the most tentative explanation has been advanced, nor the utter bewilderment with which Chur-chur announced his initial findings that day.

He had hurriedly converted himself to a convenient size to permit actual entry into the stranger's body.

When he emerged, he stood in silence for several minutes. Then, very slowly, he said:

'I have examined the 'central brain' in the forepart of his body. It is no more than a simple auxiliary computer mechanism. It does not possess the slightest trace of consciousness. And there is no other conceivable center of intelligence in the remainder of his body.' There is something I wish I could forget. I can't explain why it should upset me so much. But I always stop the tape before it reaches the point where the voice of the stranger rises in pitch, going higher and higher until it cuts out.

There's a quality about that noise that makes me tremble and think of rust.

Isaac Asimov
But I, too, Am a Robot

Isaac Asimov (1919–1992) was one of the most acclaimed science-fiction authors of the 20th century. Together with Arthur C. Clarke and Robert A. Heinlein he is often referred to as one of the Big Three of science fiction. Born to Jewish parents in Russia, he spent most of his childhood in New York where he first came into contact with science-fiction stories in his father's candy store, which sold magazines and newspapers besides candy. He graduated in chemistry at the age of 19. After the Second World War, he became a university teacher but gave this up in the early 1950s to become a full-time writer. Apart from science-fiction novels and short stories, Asimov also published pieces of crime fiction and a considerable number of non-fiction books. His most famous works include the Foundation Series and the Robot series. His science-fiction story *Nightfall* (1941), about the coming of darkness on a planet with eternal sunlight, was voted the best short science-fiction story of all time by the Science Fiction Writers of America in 1964. Asimov is also famous for his Three Laws of Robotics introduced in his 1942 short story *Runaround*. The following excerpt is taken from the novelette *The Bicentennial Man,* which was first published in 1976.

What does it mean to be human? Which characteristics are necessary to qualify as a person?

Read Asimov's Three Laws of Robotics:

- *First Law: A robot may not injure a human being, or, through inaction, allow a human being to come to harm.*
- *Second Law: A robot must obey the orders given it by human beings except where such orders would conflict with the first law.*
- *Third Law: A robot must protect its own existence as long as such protection does not conflict with the First or Second Law.*

What is your opinion of the laws? What status does Asimov assign to robots?

1.

Andrew Martin said, 'Thank you,' and took the seat offered him. He didn't look driven to the last resort[1], but he had been.

He didn't, actually, look anything, for there was a smooth blankness, to his face, except for the sadness one imagined one saw in his eyes. His hair was smooth, light brown, rather fine; and he had no facial hair. He looked freshly and cleanly shaved. His clothes were distinctly[2] old-fashioned, but neat, and predominantly[3] a velvety[4] red-purple in color.

Facing him from behind the desk was the surgeon[5]. The nameplate on the desk included a fully identifying series of letters and numbers which Andrew didn't bother with. To call him Doctor would be quite enough.

'When can the operation be carried through, Doctor?' he asked.

Softly, with that certain inalienable note of respect that a robot always used to a human being, the surgeon said, 'I am not certain, sir, that I understand how or upon whom such an operation could be performed.'

There might have been a look of respectful intransigence[6] on the surgeon's face, if a robot of his sort, in lightly bronzed stainless steel, could have such an expression – or any expression.

Andrew Martin studied the robot's right hand, his cutting hand, as it lay motionless on the desk. The fingers were long and were shaped into artistically metallic, looping[7] curves so graceful and appropriate that one could imagine a scalpel fitting them and becoming, temporarily, one piece with them. There would be no hesitation in his work, no stumbling[8], no quivering[9], no mistakes. That confidence came with specialization, of course, a specialization so fiercely desired by humanity that few robots were, any longer,

1 last resort: *letzter Ausweg* **2** distinctly: clearly **3** predominantly: mostly **4** velvety: *samten* **5** surgeon: *Chirurg/in* **6** intransigence: *Uneinsichtigkeit, Unnachgiebigkeit* **7** looping: *Schleifen ausführend* **8** stumbling (n): *Versehen* **9** quivering: shaking

independently brained. A surgeon, of course, would have to be. But this one, though brained, was so limited in his capacity that he did not recognize Andrew, had probably never heard of him.

'Have you ever thought you would like to be a man?' Andrew asked.

The surgeon hesitated a moment, as though the question fitted nowhere in his allotted[1] positronic pathways[2]. 'But I am a robot, sir.'

'Would it be better to be a man?'

'If would be better, sir, to be a better surgeon. I could not be so if I were a man, but only if I were a more advanced robot. I would be pleased to be a more advanced robot.'

'It does not offend you that I can order you about? That I can make you stand up, sit down, move right or left, by merely telling you to do so?'

'It is my pleasure to please you, sir. If your orders were to interfere with my functioning with respect to you or to any other human being, I would not obey you. The First Law, concerning my duty to human safety, would take precedence over[3] the Second Law relating to obedience. Otherwise, obedience is my pleasure. Now, upon whom am I to perform this operation?'

'Upon me,' Andrew said.

'But that is impossible. It is patently[4] a damaging operation.'

'That does not matter,' said Andrew, calmly.

'I must not inflict damage[5],' said the surgeon.

'On a human being, you must not,' said Andrew, 'but I, too, am a robot.'

1 allotted: *zugewiesen* **2** pathway: *Leitbahn* **3** take precedence over sb./sth.: *Vorrang haben gegenüber jdm./etwas* **4** patently: clearly **5** inflict damage on sb./sth.: *jdm./etwas Schaden zufügen*

2.

Andrew had appeared much more a robot when he had first been – manufactured. He had then been as much a robot in appearance as any that had ever existed, smoothly designed and functional.

He had done well in the home to which he had been brought in those days when robots in households, or on the planet altogether, had been a rarity. There had been four in the home: Sir and Ma'am and Miss and Little Miss. He knew their names, of course, but he never used them. Sir was Gerald Martin.

His own serial number was NDR– He eventually forgot the numbers. It had been a long time, of course; but if he had wanted to remember, he could not have forgotten. He had not wanted to remember.

Little Miss had been the first to call him Andrew, because she could not use the letters, and all the rest followed her in this.

Little Miss – She had lived for ninety years and was long since dead. He had tried to call her Ma'am once, but she would not allow it. Little Miss she had been to her last day.

Andrew had been intended to perform the duties of a valet, a butler, even a lady's maid. Those were the experimental days for him and, indeed, for all robots anywhere save in the industrial and exploratory factories and stations off Earth.

The Martins enjoyed him, and half the time he was prevented from doing his work because Miss and Little Miss wanted to play with him. It was Miss who first understood how this might be arranged. 'We order you to play with us and you must follow orders.'

'I am sorry, Miss, but a prior order from Sir must surely take precedence.'

But she said, 'Daddy just said he hoped you would take care of the cleaning. That's not much of an order. I order you.'

Sir did not mind. Sir was fond of Miss and of Little Miss, even more than Ma'am was; and Andrew was fond of them, too. At least, the effect they had upon his actions were those which in a human being would have been called the result of fondness[1]. Andrew thought of it as fondness for he did not know any other word for it.

It was for Little Miss that Andrew had carved[2] a pendant[3] out of wood. She had ordered him to. Miss, it seemed, had received an ivorite[4] pendant with scrollwork[5] for her birthday and Little Miss was unhappy over it. She had only a piece of wood, which she gave Andrew together with a small kitchen knife.

He had done it quickly and Little Miss had said, 'That's *nice,* Andrew. I'll show it to Daddy.'

Sir would not believe it. 'Where did you really get this, Mandy?' Mandy was what he called Little Miss. When Little Miss assured him she was really telling the truth, he turned to Andrew. 'Did you do this, Andrew?'

'Yes, Sir.'

'The design, too?'

'Yes, Sir.'

'From what did you copy the design?'

'It is a geometric representation, Sir, that fits the grain[6] of the wood.'

The next day, Sir brought him another piece of wood – a larger one – and an electric vibro-knife[7]. 'Make something out of this, Andrew. Anything you want to,' he said.

Andrew did so as Sir watched, then looked at the product a long time. After that, Andrew no longer waited on tables. He was ordered to read books on furniture design instead, and he learned to make cabinets[8] and desks.

'These are amazing productions, Andrew,' Sir soon told him.

'I enjoy doing them, Sir,' Andrew admitted.

'Enjoy?'

1 fondness: affection **2** carve sth.: *etwas schnitzen* **3** pendant: *Anhänger*
4 ivorite: made of ivory **5** scrollwork: *Verzierung* **6** grain: *Maserung*
7 vibro-knife: a special kind of knife with a vibrating blade **8** cabinet: *Kommode, Schrank*

'It makes the circuits[1] of my brain somehow flow more easily. I have heard you use the word "enjoy" and the way you use it fits the way I feel. I enjoy doing them, Sir.'

1 circuit: *Stromkreis, Schaltung*

Jeffrey McDaniel
The Quiet World

Jeffrey McDaniel was born in 1967 in Philadelphia, Pennsylvania. He began publishing poems at university. Since then, he has published five books of poetry; the poem 'The Quiet World' first appeared in his collection *The Forgiveness Parade* (1998). Since 2001, he has been teaching creative writing at a college in Yonkers, New York.

In an effort to get people to look
into each other's eyes more,
and also to appease[1] the mutes[2],
the government has decided
to allot[3] each person exactly one hundred
and sixty-seven words, per day.

When the phone rings, I put it to my ear
without saying hello. In the restaurant
I point at chicken noodle soup.
I am adjusting well to the new way.

Late at night, I call my long distance lover,
proudly say *I only used fifty-nine today.*
I saved the rest for you.

When she doesn't respond,
I know she's used up all her words,
so I slowly whisper *I love you*
thirty-two and a third times.
After that, we just sit on the line
and listen to each other breathe.

1 appease sb.: make sb. calm down **2** mute: person who cannot speak **3** allot sth. to sb.: *jdm. etwas zuweisen*

ADDITIONAL TEXT

AN OVERVIEW OF THE GENRES

This overview is intended to provide a small insight into the world of speculative fiction and to help you find your way around when exploring some of the imagined worlds in science fiction. For reasons of space the present overview ignores all the other sub-genres that exist. While it is generally agreed upon that a distinction has to be made between speculative fiction and non-speculative fiction, all other divisions depend on your understanding of a specific genre. Speculative fiction are stories that speculate about how things may be, and about things that may not have happened but which may indeed happen.

The genre of science-fiction alone is incredibly complex and can be divided in an almost uncountable number of sub-genres, all of which deal with their own specific themes. Generally speaking, a distinction can be made between hard and soft science fiction. While the former has a clear emphasis on science, the latter focusses more on the plot and the characters of the story. In other words, hard science fiction answers the question of "how" and soft science fiction deal with the "why".

Moreover, any of the genres listed on the page opposite can easily cross the boundaries of other genres and by doing so establish a completely new genre. Many of the examples in this collection of texts are either science fiction or (young adult) dystopian narratives. Yet it is difficult, if not impossible, to offer a clear-cut distinction between these two genres. Some consider dystopian fiction and their young adult counterparts a sub-genre of science fiction, as they describe a hypothetical, (as yet) non-existent world. What happens, however, if a story describes a dystopian world without any reference to science or scientific advancements? Does it still count as science fiction? One further example to illustrate the crux of the problem: many dystopias take place in an apocalyptic world, for example Sacci Lloyd's *Carbon Diaries*, or post-apocalyptic world, for example Julia Bertagna's *Exodus*. The question is, however, what then makes dystopian fiction different from post-apocalyptic fiction. Well, one answer could be that post-apocalyptic fiction centres more around the individual's fight for survival in a hostile environment while dystopian fiction tends to focus more on the individual's fight against the dark forces of a totalitarian state. When reading the texts in this collection, you will notice that most, if not all of them, blend themes and elements from two or even more genres and, although they do not fit into traditional genre boxes, they offer a unique reading experience.

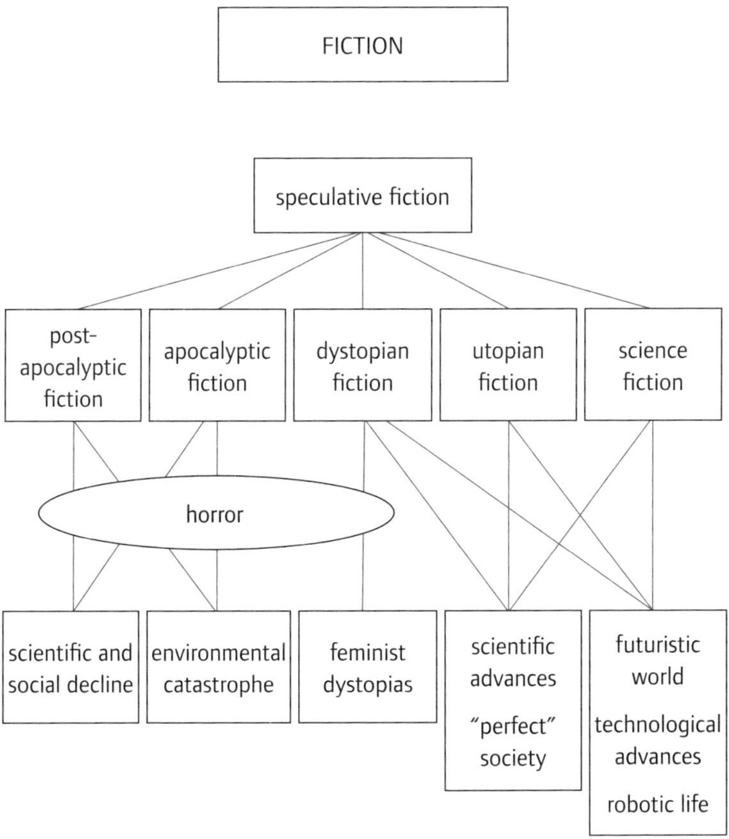

QUELLENVERZEICHNIS

ABBILDUNGEN:

S. 28: Saci Lloyd Carbon Rationing. In: The Carbon Diaries. First published in Great Britain in 2008 by Hodder Children's Books, an imprint of Hachette Children's group, Part of Hodder and Stoughton, London 2008 – **S. 78–83:** © 2017 by Connor Willumsen

TEXTE:

S. 9: Peter Payack: The Migration of Darkness. In: Roger Dutcher/Mike Allen (2005): *The Alchemy of Stars*. Published by SFPA 2005 – **S. 11:** Julie Bertagna: The Rising Waves. In: *Exodus*. First published 2002 by Young Picador, an imprint of Pan Macmillan Ltd; reissued by Macmillan Children's Books. London 2011 – **S. 23:** Saci Lloyd Carbon Rationing. In: *The Carbon Diaries*. First published in Great Britain in 2008 by Hodder Children's Books, an imprint of Hachette Children's group, Part of Hodder and Stoughton, London 2008 – **S. 31:** James Tiptree, Jr.: The Girl Who Was Plugged in. Copyright © 1973 by James Tiptree Jr. Veröffentlicht mit Genehmigung Nr. 71'727 der Paul & Peter Fritz AG in Zürich – **S. 77:** Connor Willumsen: A Journey through a Dystopian Future. In: *Anti-Gone*. First Published by Koyama Press. Toronto 2017 – **S. 84:** Ray Bradbury: A Sound of Thunder. Reprinted by permission of Don Congdon Associates, Inc. Copyright © 1952 by the Crowell Collier Publishing Company, renewed 1980 by Ray Bradbury – **S. 99:** Ursula Le Guin: Solitude. Copyright © 1994 by Ursula K. Le Guin First appeared in "The Magazine of Fantasy and Science Fiction" in 1994, then in *The Birthday of the World* published by HarperCollins in 2002, and later appeared in *The Unreal and the Real* published by Small Beer Press in 2012.Reprinted by permission of Curtis Brown, Ltd. – **S. 133:** Peter Phillips: Lost Memory. In: *Galaxy Science Fiction* May 1952 – **S. 148:** Isaac Asimov: But I, too, Am a Robot. In: The Bicentennial Man from Isaac Asimov: COMPLETE STORIES, VOLUME 2 by Isaac Asimov, © 1992 by Isaac Asimov. Used by permission of Doubleday, an imprint of the Knopf Doubleday Publishing Group, a division of Penguin Random House LLC. All rights reserved. – **S. 154:** Jeffrey McDaniel: The Quiet World from *The Forgiveness Parade*. Manic D Press, 1998.